CAROL VAN KLOMPENBURG

What To Do When You Can't Do It All

Coming to Terms with Overcommitment

AUGSBURG Publishing House • Minneapolis

WHAT TO DO WHEN YOU CAN'T DO IT ALL
Coming to Terms with Overcommitment

Scripture quotations unless otherwise noted are from the Holy Bible: New International Version. Copyright 1978 by the New York International Bible Society. Used by permission of Zondervan Bible Publishers.

The excerpt on page 40 from C. S. Lewis (*Perelandra*, New York: MacMillan, 1944) is reprinted by permission of the Estate of C. S. Lewis.

The excerpt on pages 90-91 from Josef Pieper (*Leisure: the Basis of Culture*. Trans. Alexander Dru, New York: Random House, 1964) is reprinted by permission of Pantheon Books, a Division of Random House, Inc.

The material on page 117 from James Schaap (*Home Free*, Westchester, IL: Crossway Books, 1986) is reprinted by permission of James Schaap.

The excerpt on pages 123-124 from Robert Myering ("Hilarity: More Than a Minor Virtue," *Christian Home and School*, May/June 1986) is reprinted by permission of Christian Schools International.

The poem "T.T.T." on page 142 by Piet Hein is reprinted from *Grooks* (Garden City, NY: Doubleday & Company Inc., 1969).

The material on page 140 from James Dobson (*Hide or Seek*, Old Tappan, NJ: Fleming H. Revell, 1979) is reprinted by permission of Fleming H. Revell Company.

Library of Congress Cataloging-in-Publication Data

Van Klompenburg, Carol.
    WHAT TO DO WHEN YOU CAN'T DO IT ALL.

    1. Perfectionism (Personality trait) 2. Excellence—
Religious aspects—Christianity. 3. Christian life—
1960-   . I. Title.
BF698.35.P47V36   1988   248.4   89-100
ISBN 0-8066-2391-8

Manufactured in the U.S.A.   APH 10-7051

1   2   3   4   5   6   7   8   9   0   1   2   3   4   5   6   7   8   9

Contents

Preface

Perhaps some Christians recline on chaise lounges, eat chocolate bonbons, and watch soap operas. But I don't know them. Somewhere there may be people who rest in backyard patio chairs and listen to the grass grow. I haven't met them.

The Christians I know sag under a burden of multiple roles, each crying for excellence. The people I know want 48-hour days in order to do it all.

If you're a chocolate bonbon Christian, this book is not for you. But if, like me, you're a do-it-all person ripping at the seams as you stretch to achieve, read on.

Already in first grade, I felt the tug of the achievement drive when I brought home a straight-A report card. I knew the hypnotic power of excelling when my first poem won a blue ribbon. Eventually I became a slave to a need to do-it-all-and-do-it-well.

In recent years, the word which has epitomized that drive is *excellence*. We feel a need to be excellent parents, spouses, homemakers, employees, church members. We want to be excellent friends, prayer warriors, conversationalists.

I began writing this book as a personal declaration of war

against that do-it-all-and-do-it-well tyrant. In the crash of battle I relearned the victory of God's gift of good enough. He accepts me as I am. I bumped against a rolled-away stone, peered into an empty tomb, and rediscovered the miracle of grace.

May that joyful surprise be yours as you journey these pages.

Acknowledgments

This book did not rise from a void; I did not do it all. It has been formed by people whose lives shape mine. To all of them, I am grateful.

I'd especially like to thank:

* My fellow do-it-all strugglers, who shared their lives with me and whose stories appear on the following pages. I have changed their names and some details of their lives to protect their privacy, but their stories are true;
* Cal Meuzelaar, who guided me in forming some crucial concepts for this book;
* Maureen Rank and Martha Popson, fellow writers whose critique and encouragement helped me find my own writing voice;
* Roland Seboldt, whose enthusiasm and deadline helped me more than he realized;
* Irene Getz and John Hanka, whose careful editing provided accuracy and polish;
* Finally, my husband Marlo, whose patient support helped to steady me through the months of being "with book."

1

The Clamor about Excellence

Laura was a woman who wanted to do it all. Her 36 years were a long tally of accomplishments: high school valedictorian, accomplished soloist, summa cum laude college degree, masters degree in English literature.

Then at midlife, a wife and a mother of four children, she found the roller coaster of her moods out of control. She felt unable to cope with parenting and often considered herself a failure as a mother. She sought help through therapy.

When, after several sessions, her counselor asked if she was doing an adequate job of parenting, she was baffled.

"By what standard?" she asked him. "By the standard of the department of social services?"

He sidestepped her question, "Do you provide for their physical needs?"

"Yes," she answered.

"You just told me about inviting friends to play with them, your reading with them, and your family outings, so I know that you provide for their social needs. Do you subject them to physical abuse or constant verbal harassment?"

"No," she said, puzzled.

"So—are you doing an adequate job?"

Laura hesitated, "Well, by the standard of social services, I suppose I am. The agency is not going to come and take my children away."

"Then, you are doing an adequate job, right?" He leaned back in his chair and linked his hands behind his head.

Anger and pain roiled within Laura and she wanted to reach over and shake him. Words wrenched themselves from her heart, as if self-powered, "But adequate isn't good enough. *It just isn't good enough,*" she answered.

Laura remembers that moment as an epiphany. "I didn't realize until that instant the standard I had set for myself. Adequate was not good enough for me. To be adequate was to fail. Only excellence was acceptable—in parenting and in my whole life."

Laura wanted to do it all and do it well. Her goal was excellence in everything. And *excellence,* as author John Gardner observes, "is a curiously powerful word."

Laura is not alone. Men and women everywhere feel pressured to achieve excellence in all they do. The confusions of being a woman in today's society make women especially prone to the excellence trap.

Women today wonder whether to choose a career or a family or both, whereas there used to be no question. Psychologist Baila Zeitz observes that now, when a woman makes a choice, she feels a compulsion to be very good at it—whatever the choice.

In their role as homemakers, women have the added pressure of being generalists in a world of increasing specialization. Each specialist clamors for more attention. Julia Childs demonstrates gourmet meals. *Good Housekeeping* pictures perfect houses. And James Dobson teaches successful childraising.

When I browsed two family magazines recently, they trapped me in parental guilt. In the first, a mother whose 13-year-old daughter had now read 100 classics suggested keeping books in every room of the house, togetherness trips to the library, reading the classics aloud, and setting a good example by reading them yourself. In the second article, a woman, whose 11-year-old son had recognized a missed note in a performance of Bach's Brandenburg Concerto No. 6, recommended frequent exposure to good music.

I felt like a failure. My oldest son devours Garfield and Peanuts cartoon books, not classics. And my second son's report card rated him deficient in holding pitch. Neither of them has read 25 classics and neither has heard Bach's Brandenburg Concerto No. 6 once.

Let's face it. Women who set out to excel as wives, mothers, and homemakers have a tall mountain to climb. And if they choose to work away from home, they've raised its peak above the cloud line.

Men, too, are constantly bombarded with the excellence question. Corporate advertising is thick with excellence slogans. Even the Marines don't want just anybody. Give them "a few good men."

How tall is your excellence mountain? To find out, take a few minutes to answer the following questions.

T F 1) My evaluation of myself rides a roller coaster which ranges from "I can conquer the world" to "I can't do anything right."

T F 2) I feel like a failure when I make mistakes.

T F 3) For me, being adequate is not enough.

T F 4) I often compare myself to other people on a vertical scale, checking if I am better or worse than them at a certain skill.

T F 5) I rarely complete my "to do" list for a day.

T F 6) Doing an excellent job gives me more worth and value.

T F 7) For me, getting to the goal is more important than enjoying the moment.

T F 8) God expects me to always do my best for him.

T   F   9) My parents set high standards for me when I was
a child.

T   F   10) When I refer to someone as a perfectionist, I am
praising him or her.

Now count the number of statements you labeled true. If
you answered more than three statements as true, you may be
a slave to excellence. And your emotional roller coaster may
be resulting from your attitude toward achievement.

We are a country with a compulsion. All around us a
cacaphony of voices summons us to excellence in everything.

In his landmark book, *Excellence,* John Gardner cried out
for excellence, "We need excellent physicists and excellent con-
struction workers, excellent legislators and excellent first-grade
teachers. The tone and fiber of our society depend upon a
pervasive, almost universal striving for good performance."

In *A Passion for Excellence,* Tom Peters and Nancy Austin
wrote, "Even a pocket of excellence can fill your life like a
wall-to-wall revolution. We have found that the majority of
passionate activists who hammer away at the old boundaries
have given up family vacations, Little League games, birthday
dinners, evenings, weekends and lunch hours, gardening,
reading, movies and most other pastimes."

Now stop a moment and check your emotional pulse. After
hearing these clamoring voices, how do you feel?

There's a good chance your emotional level is about "D"
right now. You could be feeling either driven or defeated. If
you're feeling that way, take heart. Some people have escaped
those demanding voices.

To start that escape process, jot down answers to these
questions.

1) Define excellence.

2) Is excellence important to you? How important? More
important than what? Less important than what?

3) Why is excellence important?

Before you read the next paragraph, stop! Did you really

answer the questions above, or did you simply read them? If you did not answer them, please try again.

Do you still have a blank sheet of paper or a blank mind? Is it hard for you to say how important excellence is to you, to state why it's important and to define it?

Answering those questions may be difficult because to answer them is to expose excellence-in-everything as the wolf cry that it is. For slaves of excellence, defining it is like submerging their hands in a bowl of Jello to find its shape. And so is explaining the importance of and basis for excellence. We have accepted it as a standard without examining or understanding it.

Not everyone accepts the clamor for excellence, however. Marcia, like Laura, is a bright, midlife mother. She sat across from me at her slightly smudged table one morning, leaned forward with her blue stoneware mug cradled between her hands, and said, "If the Lord wanted to send me children and said to me, 'Now, Marcia, you do an excellent job of raising these kids,' I'd say to him 'Huh-uh, don't send me any kids, Lord, thank you.' But if he said to me, 'Do an adequate job of raising them,' I'd say, 'OK, Lord, I'll give it a try.' "

The clamor for excellence in everything is not just in our society. The voices are also inside us. North American Christians accept the excellence standard. We meekly nod our heads to the voices demanding it.

Do the "tone and fiber of our society" really depend "upon a pervasive, almost universal striving for good performance?" Is excellence really worth giving up "family vacations, Little League games, birthday dinners, evenings . . . "? No! That message is a lie! We have sold our birthright of good enough for the mess of excellence pottage, without even knowing the ingredients of the stew.

2

The Confusion about Excellence

Sue is really an excellent teacher," said Kate.

Curious, I asked her, "Kate, what do you mean when you say excellent?"

She paused a moment, and finally answered with a flicker of anger, "I don't know."

Her irritation puzzled me. I had really wanted to know. I had not intended to embarrass her.

But she had no ready answer for my question. She had not sorted out the meanings of excellence. Neither have many other do-it-all people.

The measurement of excellence—even in a simple tennis match—requires an agreed-upon standard. We could set up various scoring systems for excellence in tennis. We could simply measure who makes a higher percentage of backhand strokes, who has more speed on her serve, or whose smash is more consistent, but we don't. We could also measure by who smiles more often, or who compliments the other person on a good shot more often, but we don't. We have agreed on a point-scoring method for determining the winner.

In life, however, we don't always agree on scoring methods. When we think of excellence we have a mix of meanings. In parenting, one person's harshness is another's firm discipline. One's patience is judged as passivity by another. One mother's nurturing seems to another overly protective. One mother's relaxed housekeeping is another's slovenliness. I may call it creative freedom, but my friend may call it chaos. I may call it flexible, but my husband may call it wishy-washy.

Many of the same contradictory standards for excellence *among* us are also *within* each of us: We have internalized the contradictions. My standards tell me to win, but at the same time to put others first. They tell me to be a model parent, but to fulfill my (almost) infinite potential. I believe I should become rich, and yet live simply in order to give to the poor.

The varied meanings of excellence can be sorted into four groups. Let's imagine a different person to match each meaning.

Sue is an excellent teacher. She is compassionate, firm, bright, creative, organized, articulate, knowledgeable, and hard-working. Because she has most of these ideal qualities, she is an excellent teacher. She comes close to the perfect model.

Sue's colleague Joe has just won the state Coach of the Year award. In the past five years his basketball teams have gone to state tournaments four times. Their win-loss ratio is 9 to 1.

Bob's business is unusually profitable. He started 20 years ago with a $600 dollar loan from the local bank, and now his net annual income exceeds $200,000. He is a board member at the same bank which loaned him that first $600.

His wife Diane jogs, attends aerobic classes, studies piano, and takes a painting class. She attends a weekly Bible study and is a member of a support group. She has just reentered school to begin her master's program.

Sue, John, Bob, and Diane match different models for excellence. Sue's excellence means *coming close to the perfect model* or ideal. John's excellence lies in *beating out the competition*. Bob's excellence at business has provided him a *path to success*—to money, power, and prestige. Diane aims for excellence by trying to *achieve her full potential*.

Each of these four concepts provides fuel for our excellence drive.

Matching the ideal

If I want to do an excellent job of parenting, I may have an ideal in mind. A perfect mother never yells at her children, and she rarely leaves them with a baby-sitter. She always makes homemade snacks and attractive, nutritious meals. She dresses her children well, preferably in handmade clothing. She runs an orderly house where the toys are put away soon after play, but she allows free range for creativity. She never runs out of energy, never feels blue.

She is unselfish and puts her children's needs before her own. She plays educational games with them and reads to them daily. She understands each stage of child development, and carefully readies her children for each new stage. She trains them to obey instantly, but without fear.

Having established that ideal model of the perfect mother, I go about trying to live up to it. On those rare moments when I approach my ideal, I feel I am an excellent mother.

Similarly, I can model myself after the ideal Christian. The model Christian is never too tired for another job in his church. He spends an hour in prayer and meditation each morning, attends Bible studies, and does volunteer work at the nursing home. He attends two worship services each Sunday, sings in church choir, teaches Sunday school, plays on the church softball team, and does door-to-door canvassing. When I approximate this model, I am an excellent Christian.

Beating the competition

But a perfect model is not the excellence standard for everyone. My friend Marilyn defines *excellence* as a two-letter ending. She explains, "*Excellence* is defined by the suffix '-er.' I was brought up with a need to be smarter, richer, neater. It wasn't enough to get good grades; they had to be better than those of someone else. It wasn't enough to earn money; it had to be more than the neighbors earned."

The competitive definition of excellence is most clearly seen in sports, and exemplified by an ad featuring tennis star Martina Navratilova next to the motto, "Whoever said winning isn't everything, probably lost." When I play tennis, I agree with my opponent that whoever scores the most points wins the game. Beating my opponent is my measure for excellence.

Some Christians follow this theme with mottoes like, "God never made man to come in second place." We use it when we say God wants us to win.

As modern technology has shrunk our world, it has expanded our field of competition. My great-grandmother could enjoy local soloists without comparing them to professionals recorded on compact disc. I can't. School plays compete with "Masterpiece Theater." Local pastors are measured against TV's polished pulpiteers.

Competition, rather than perfection, can fuel my drive for excellent mothering. If my neighbor has taught her child to read by his fourth birthday, I want to teach mine to read by his third. If her infant started to walk at ten months, I want mine to toddle at nine. And if my friends start their children in swimming lessons at half a year, I try to start mine at three months.

If my acquaintances spend 15 minutes a day reading to their children, I aim for 20. If they start their children on piano lessons, I start mine on piano, with a touch of violin.

If I hear my neighbor screaming at her children, I make sure I speak softly and with patience in her presence the next time mine fail to toe the mark. If my sister-in-law makes homemade granola, I make granola and homemade bread. Doing a better job of mothering than my acquaintances makes me an excellent mother.

Path to success

The third framework for excellence is utilitarian: excellence is a useful tool to achieve a goal, usually the goal of success. You run an excellent business in order to make a fortune. You set your sights on a management job because it pays a better salary, and gives you more status and power in the company. You become a top-notch actress in order to be famous, admired, and envied. You work hard at politics in order to grasp the power of the presidency, or at least a governorship.

Success in our society is most frequently measured by acquiring the closely linked trio of money, power, and prestige. Millionaire J. D. Rockefeller said, "I believe that the power to make money is a gift of God." Today's Christians go a step further when they use the motto: "God wants you rich."

The Success Fantasy author Anthony Campolo analyzes it this way: "To become followers of Jesus means for the propagators of the success theology that Christians will be champions in athletics, winners in races for political office, victorious in beauty contests and leaders in business. They argue that the Christian life-style is a guaranteed route to the financial rewards that belong to the elite."

Some pastors and churches use a different strain of the prosperity gospel. The measure of excellent pastoring is huge increases in church membership. Excellent pastoring becomes a tool for that goal. One pastor friend told me, "At seminary we were taught that good pastoring resulted in rapidly expanding churches. We believed it. I set a goal of 100 people for my first church meeting in New England. When only 50 people came, I was ready to leave the ministry. I later learned that 14 of the 28 members of my graduating class had dropped from the pastorate by the end of their first year."

Achieving full potential

Andrew Rooney uses the fourth standard for excellence—personal growth—in his light-hearted sketch, "Self-Improvement Week." He decides to read one good book a week, stop eating so much, and take up jogging. He will give up TV, get more sleep, and take courses in shorthand, bookkeeping, and computers. He also plans to become more careful about his clothes and organize his time better. He concludes, "After I jog and eat my grapefruit and do my exercises and brush my teeth and read the newspaper, press my pants and cut my fingernails, I'm going to take a few minutes to relax, meditate and plan my day. I read somewhere that everyone should plan his day in advance and not just start out willy-nilly in the morning so that's what I'll do.

"I'm just sick and tired of myself the way I am. In the near future, if I follow these plans I'm making to improve myself, I'm going to be smart, efficient, muscular and in beautiful shape. I can hardly wait to see myself in the mirror."

We laugh at Rooney's self-portrait. We laugh because his portrait is a mirror in which we see ourselves.

John Gardner is an articulate proponent of excellence as fulfilling your potential. "What we must reach for," he writes in *Excellence*, "is a conception of perpetual self-discovery, perpetual reshaping to realize one's best self, to be the person one could be. . . . It isn't a question of whether the individual gets to the peak of the pyramid. We can't all get to the peak, and that isn't the point of life anyway. The question is whether individuals, whatever their worldly success, have continued to learn and grow and try."

Christians echo his theme. Ted Engstrom, in *The Pursuit of Excellence*, refers to average men and women as underachievers. He says, "If you are willing to be the person you were meant to be, I think you will discover that *for you* the sky is the limit. . . . Excellence demands that you be better than yourself."

Clashes in daily life

Analyzing these four views of excellence may help our intellectual understanding without providing much direction for life. The meanings mix and overlap in daily experience. I may wish to do excellent work not only to become rich, but also to be richer than my neighbor. I may aim for ideal motherhood, and want to come closer to that ideal than my sister.

These differing definitions of excellence may be on a collision course. They may make doing it all impossible. Excellent parenting doesn't provide a path to money or prestige in our society. (You may, however, be able to find pockets of prestige among the dedicated parents who envy your patience or your three-year-old's precocious vocabulary.)

Living as the ideal mother won't earn you the excellence of fulfilling your "sky's the limit" potential either, and it may usurp time that you could use becoming a bionic believer. You may not be able to spend 40 hours per week in volunteer work at the safe-house for abused women or lead daily neighborhood Bible studies.

Developing each of your potentials doesn't allow you time to devote 60 hours per week to your profession. Climbing over colleagues to get to the vice-presidency doesn't win you the Humanitarian of the Year Award. If your ideal person always puts the wants of others first, how can you put forth the extra effort needed to win the tennis match?

With these contradictions about what is good, we try to possess goodness "in an imminent or unusual degree." Trying to achieve excellence with such a mix of meanings is like flooring a gas pedal at a crossroads—with the transmission in neutral. It is like trying to run the 100-yard dash through a thicket.

3

The Costs of Perfectionism

If you refuse to accept anything but the best, you will get it more often." This week's Ten-Second Editorial in the company newsletter meets Doug's approval. He smiles and nods. Doug wants the best, and he knows what that means for him. He wants to be company president before he turns 50.

Doug has shifted from neutral into high gear. He knows his standard for excellence. He doesn't need to do it all. He has narrowed his field, and there only the best will do.

So has Linda. Linda has a master's degree and has begun work on her doctorate. Her standard for excellence is intellectual. To be respectable, an action has to contribute toward the growth of understanding. She needs up-to-date information. Her ideas must be clearly stated and logically developed.

Doug and Linda know *what* excellence means for them. Given a little time, they could also tell you *why* it is important. "Who wants to be just one of the staff?" says Doug. "I want more than that. Why be a serf when you have a chance to be a lord? Might as well aim for the top, and have some financial security, too. I want to do something with my life, to make my life count."

Linda says, "Ignorance is not bliss; it is nonexistence. I don't want to live in darkness. I want to know everything I can. If I understand my life and my world, I can be a more valuable member of society."

Why do Doug and Linda set high standards? Why are they compelled to excel? Because they want to be worth something. Doug looks for worth in the company presidency. Linda seeks it in being informed and knowledgeable.

When Doug was 10 he had one pair of shoes, and those had broken laces. His pants were hand-me-downs from his older brothers. His father was a blue-collar worker on minimum wage, and his mother babysat neighborhood children for extra income. He remembers his mother crying one Christmas because she couldn't afford to buy the pair of roller skates he wanted.

Once he overheard a classmate say, "Doug might be OK, if he'd get a real barber haircut and wear clothes with a little class." He promised himself that someday he'd be able to afford class.

Linda's precocity was her parent's pride.. Her mother loved to tell about the dozen nursery rhymes Linda could recite by the time she was 18 months. Besides being bright, Linda had also been a gangly adolescent with teeth which seemed several sizes too large. At the sixth grade skating party, she was the last girl standing at the wall during the couples' skate. She thought her appearance rated F, and she made up for it with a report card that rated A. The guys didn't ask her to skate, but they did ask her for help with chemistry.

The coin of worth Doug and Linda want has two sides. For Doug, the presidency will take away the patched blue jeans and the shoes with holes and will make him good enough to be accepted, to be secure, to be loved. Linda's insight compensates for her appearance. If she can be brilliant, perhaps people will forget the absence of chin and cheekbones.

But, Doug and Linda hope that the presidency and the doctorate will do even more than that. Doug wants power over his coworkers, and Linda wants people to stand in awe of her knowledge. The world, or at least their acquaintances, will envy or look up to them. They not only want to be loved, they want to be admired. They want to be acceptable—and outstanding. They want to be good enough—and excellent too.

Does the drive for excellence accomplish either of these purposes? Can it, first of all, earn acceptance and love?

Instead of giving him the security and love and acceptance he craves, Doug's standards keep people at a distance. His acquaintances and colleagues have become his competition, racing company hurdles against him to get to the finish line first. Or they become his track shoes—equipment to help him get there faster.

High standards can result in just the opposite of loving acceptance—isolation and loneliness. If Doug feels he needs to achieve in order to be loved, and sets those same standards for others, he has no one to hold his hand when business deals fall through. He feels he is only worthy of love when he succeeds. He finds it hard to accept the failures of others as well. His wife and children must earn his love. It is conditional.

Linda's standards produce the same isolation. She has little patience with a poorly articulated concept or a weak premise at Bible study groups, and points out flawed thinking with skill. Conversations become debates. She, too, fails to find the love she seeks.

Instead of enhancing relationships, the obsession with excellence may atrophy them. Relationships are colored by fear of others, criticism of them, or competition with them, all of which place relationships in a straight jacket. Psychologist Dr. David Stoops finds that people who blight their lives with goals too high are likeliest to suffer from troubled personal relationships and low self-esteem. Depression often results.

Doug and Linda are not seeking only love and acceptance; they also want the flip side of the coin of worth—power and admiration. They want to be *somebody,* not just anybody. Somebody out of the ordinary. Somebody different, somebody special, somebody outstanding.

Ironically, their strong drive to achieve may be counterproductive. If they refuse to accept anything but the best, they may get it *less* often. Although we believe that a drive for excellence leads to higher achievement, too high a drive may reduce effectiveness.

Psychologist David Burns had high standards for a graduate paper he was researching and writing. He painstakingly researched, wrote, and finally completed it. Then he realized that his colleagues had published several competent papers in the time he needed to complete just one.

Dr. Burns counseled a history professor who refused to give up his perfectionist standards, who thumbed his nose at being average. But, says Burns, his perfectionism made him less effective than many of his colleagues.

In other studies, Dr. Burns found a similar pattern. In a group of insurance agents he studied, the perfectionists (people with high standards for whom achievement determines worth) actually earned an average of $15,000 less per year than the nonperfectionists. Gymnasts who qualify for the Olympics have fewer perfectionist tendencies than those who fail to qualify.

For some people, high standards trigger procrastination. "I'm a perfectionist, but you'd never know it from my house. It is a clutter of projects I intend to finish—when I have time to do them perfectly," says my friend Donna. "And you can tell other perfectionists when you ride down the street. They are the ones with yards, like ours, that look as if they are waiting to do them until they have time to do the job just right."

Fear of not landscaping a yard or decorating a room well enough leads to putting off the work or leaving it half-finished. If the job is not completed, it is beyond criticism.

Grand expectations can be especially paralyzing in midlife, when you realize you will not achieve your youthful dreams. You will probably never write that best-selling novel. You will not win a Nobel prize for your science research. You will not star at the Metropolitan Opera, or even appear on the "Tonight Show."

If it doesn't paralyze you, perfectionism can narrow your horizons. "There are many possibilities in my life that I have not explored because I don't do them well," says Maureen. "And if I can't do something well, I leave it alone."

It can also inhibit creativity and spontaneity. After all, creativity requires a sense of play, the freedom to explore options, and the right to fail. If excellence is a constant standard, that freedom to play and to fail disappears.

Finally, perfectionism can lower achievement by contributing to health problems. It has been linked to tendencies toward heart attacks, substance abuse, and anorexia.

Suppose, however, that Doug and Linda are not compulsive enough, not perfectionist enough, for these results of their excellence drive to be apparent. They achieve the presidency and the top-of-the-class doctorate. Are they then accomplishing their purpose? Does excellence give them the power and admiration they want? Doug would like to see his high school class president ask him for a job. Linda would like to show her doctoral certificate to her sixth grade classmates who were at the skating rink.

However, the drive for power and admiration is hard to satisfy. Therapist Daniel Klaasen asked a perfectionist to imagine herself achieving her standard for being a good wife. "What would you do if you reached that goal?" he asked.

She imagined herself reaching the goal, opened her eyes, and said to him with surprise, "I'd raise it!"

Aiming for perfection is walking toward a mirage. Perfection simply doesn't exist. No window is ever free from every speck of dust. No idea is ever perfectly articulated. "To talk about the need for perfection in man is to talk about the need for another species," says Norman Cousins.

Even aiming for our best doesn't work. Our best performance is possible only once in a lifetime. That condemns us to calling ourselves failures every other time we perform that task. We rate anything less than our best not good enough.

We cope with our failure to reach our goals with a series of "if onlys." If only I could stop thinking poorly of myself. If only I had a better memory. If only I could make this one large sale. If only I could keep all 10 commandments. Then I would arrive.

The obsession with excellence is like a cat chasing her tail. It is a hike up an infinite mountain.

Both the need for acceptance and the need for power are insatiable when excellence is the tool to achieve them. The drive for excellence is a repeat performance of the Garden of Eden. It is the serpent and the fig leaves all over again.

In our drive for admiration, respect, or power, we want to be at the top. We want the control. We want the respect, adoration, and worship. We want to be God. What did the serpent say to Adam and Eve? "You shall be as God." Both serpent and excellence appeal to pride, the fundamental sin. Pride was then the appeal of the forbidden fruit, and it is now an appeal of excellence.

After the fruit came the fig leaves. When Adam and Eve saw what weak, needy creatures they had become, they used fig leaves to hide from each other and from God. Perhaps the fig leaves would hide their condition and make them acceptable. We use the fig leaves of achievement to hide our insecurities. Excellence is simply a different kind of covering. Wearing it, we walk through the world with imposter complexes, afraid we'll be discovered for the imperfect, needy people we are.

By shifting into high gear and heading for excellence, Doug, Linda, and all compulsive excellence seekers bite Eden's forbidden fruit and dress in fig leaves again. We both repeat the original sin of pride and hide its effect on us.

However, when we head for excellence, we know deep inside that by eternal standards we cannot be excellent. We cannot even be good enough.

Ever since the fall—the first attempt to be God—we have not been good enough. All have sinned and fallen short of the glory of God, the Bible tells us, and even our best works are hay and stubble. We cannot earn worth by striving for excellence, not with a million dollars or a million good works.

Doug and Linda, and the rest of us excellence seekers, are on a continuous roller coaster ride. We're dependent, not self-sufficient. We are creatures, not Creator. That job's been filled. The gate to being God is locked forever.

We cannot earn God's acceptance and love either. But there is another path to that goal, a path of grace provided through our Savior, Jesus Christ.

4

The Gift of Good Enough

Janet sat across the table from me relaxing over a late night snack after a harried day at a writer's conference. A classic-faced woman with waist-length hair, she was acquisitions editor for a major Christian publishing house. I saw her as a sort of demi-god with life-and-death power over book proposals.

She leaned forward, stirred her coffee, and supported her chin in her palm as she said, "You know what I wish somebody would write a book on? Never enough. Because it seems that there is never enough—never enough energy, never enough talent, never enough money. It's just never enough."

I knew her pain. I had "never enoughs" in my life, too. Never enough time with my children. Never enough energy to write until midnight. Never enough drive to stick to my exercise program or my daily devotional time. Never enough skill to rise past the middle of the tennis ladder. Never enough commitment to church activities. Never enough volunteer time for my community.

Those "never enoughs" led me into the darkness of "never good enough."

One crisp October morning, a fellow Christian brought new light to my darkness. Leading devotions for 20 Christian journalists, theologian Neal Plantinga said, "The achievement ethic is a constant temptation for contemporary—and medieval—Christianity. . . . To all such stuff, to all religion as achieved acceptability, Luther first and then Calvin said a resounding no. You are not a Savior for the likes of you. We cannot get our dim lights trimmed and burning bright. None of our pathetic little housecleanings prepares us for the God who wants to take up residence in us. No. Never. You are acceptable only on God's terms, not yours."

New light broke into my never-enough world. I sat wordless, knowing that I so often tried to achieve acceptability, to get my own lights trimmed and burning bright. I sat convicted of pathetic little housecleanings. My dim light was never enough.

"The name of the game from now on," continued Plantinga (quoting Robert Capon), "is resurrection, not bookkeeping." What a relief! I did not have to pound down the door to God, or earn my way into his presence. With his scarred hands Jesus opened the door of grace, took my hand in his, and led me in.

I am no self-made woman, I am God-made. I have no basis for self-esteem other than God-esteem. And since Adam and Eve, no one has truly been able to say, "I'm OK—You're OK." We can only say, "We're not OK, but it's OK—because of Christ."

Because Jesus said, "It is finished," because his death was enough, we are good enough. Although what we do is never enough, in him we become good enough forever.

We have worth. We are good enough because through Christ we are loved by God forever.

The worth we seek so desperately by excellence in everything is a free gift, if we confess playing God and admit our need for him. We don't need to achieve worth, just accept it.

With that acceptance comes relief. Author Keith Miller

said it felt like being freed from constantly having to fit into a suit several sizes too large. Martin Luther, freed from the need to be perfect, rejoiced that he could throw himself upon God's grace.

I had learned the lesson of grace before that crisp October morning. I believed Jesus had died for me. But that morning, struggling with the need to be good enough, I realized more clearly than ever before, that grace was a gift of good enough, not something earned by working for excellence.

Because I kept confusing excellence and good enough, I was like a 16-year-old handed the keys to the car, given the right to drive, but unable to start it because she kept trying to use the house key. God had given me the vehicle of grace, but I didn't enjoy it because I was trying to use the wrong key!

When we think that striving for excellence will work, we keep the key of good-enough-through-grace in our pocket and we feel pressured. We feel pressure, thinking: I will obey God's command about coveting. I really should visit shut-ins every month. I need to do more for the church. I should get a job—or get a better job.

When we fail, our solution is to try harder. Tomorrow I will be more loving, start daily morning meditation, have more patience with my children. Next year I'll do better at my job and get that promotion, or at least deserve it. Soon I will achieve excellence.

God's grace is not a guarantee—or even a promise of excellence, in any of its four meanings. Grace doesn't empower us to excel others. God doesn't hand over money, power, and prestige. We won't be replicas of some perfect, flawless model. And we might not mushroom with personal growth.

"Stop!" you say. "God doesn't promise excellence—just good enough? You mean I'm condemned to being mediocre or average? Who wants to be mediocre or average? You're certainly not going to make a case for that, are you?"

We have an aversion for those two words. I remember the lawyer who said to me, "The worst thing that anybody can say about me is that I am a mediocre lawyer. That's the worst thing. And I don't want my children to be mediocre either."

In a church newsletter, I found Edmund Gaudet's diatribe against average:

"Average" is the top of the bottom, the best of the worst, the bottom of the top, the worst of the best. . . . Being "average" is the lazy person's cop out: it's lacking the drive to take a stand in life: it's living by default. Being "average" is to take up space for no purpose.

So we recoil from average, from mediocre, from adequate, despite knowing that for any skill, half of the population will be average or below. If being average is "to take up space for no purpose," half of the world serves no purpose! A case could be made, I think, for average being indeed worthwhile.

But there is a better case to be made against the clamor about excellence. Below average, average, and excellent are not the only options. A world which knows only these is a world too small. It is a world which sets up an inaccurate framework.

When Jesus tells us to be perfect, "as your heavenly Father is perfect," he isn't talking about being error-free or infinite. He's talking about being mature, about fulfilling our purpose. And the form of the Greek verb used is not that of a command, but of a promise! We will fulfill our purpose.

When Paul said he could do all things through Christ who strengthened him, he was talking about ability to do his calling, not magic. Sometimes good enough may mean 99th percentile and sometimes it may mean 20th. Good enough uses a different measure, the measure of purpose.

A couple of years ago, I was asked to speak to a church society group of 30 senior citizens. Before my talk the leader opened with prayer and then asked for a volunteer to accompany group singing. To his shock all of the pianists from the group were either wintering in Florida or sick. He subsided into helpless silence. How could the group sing without their customary piano accompaniment? And how could they begin their meeting without singing?

"Are there really no piano players here tonight? Mary, you play, don't you?" Mary didn't play, and neither did Betty or Minnie.

The woman next to me glanced my way and whispered, "Do you play?"

"A little," I demurred, then changed my mind. "Well, I suppose, if there's no one else . . . "

I plunked my rusty way through three hymns, hitting a few sour chords and dropping a difficult left-hand harmony on one chorus. But the group was grateful for the service. The chairman thanked me after the singing—and again after the meeting concluded.

My skills were definitely not excellent, in fact, below average, but they were adequate for the task. My playing enabled the group to sing together as they wanted. I had been called to the job and had been good enough.

When my husband, a skilled pianist, provides the offertory for a Sunday worship service, the standard for good enough is different. Then adequate is above average. Providing offertories is not my task, but his. I am adequate for only the tasks to which God calls me.

Marcia, who wanted to do an adequate job as a parent (see Chapter 1), told me when I visited her that afternoon in her kitchen that she had made a list of what adequate meant to her. Here's Marcia's list:

Adequate means I will not fall apart when an unexpected guest walks into my uncleaned house.

Adequate means the world doesn't stand or fall by the thread of my accomplishments or failures.

Adequate means sometimes my children will be wonderful, and sometimes they will be terrible, and that is OK.

Adequate means I can like other people and enjoy them and accept them even if they are not perfect.

Adequate means that comparing myself to others is not going to tell me anything worthwhile.

Adequate means there is more than one way of doing things.

Adequate means being able to say "I am sorry" and then letting go.

Adequate means not being responsible for everyone else.

Adequate means accepting the fact that the world does not hang in the balance when I am not feeling well.

The gift of good enough leaves no room for pride. As C. S. Lewis wrote in *Mere Christianity*, "In God you come up against something which is in every respect immeasurably superior to yourself. Unless you know God as that—and therefore yourself as nothing in comparison—you do not know God at all. As long as you are proud you cannot know God."

And if you know God, you have his gift of good enough.

The importance of excellence, in any of its four meanings, fades in the bright light of good enough. Being better than others becomes irrelevant. We recognize them as our siblings and coworkers. They are different parts of Christ's body with different tasks. We recognize success as the shallow and fleeting goal it is. We realize that reaching our full potential and measuring up to some ideal are impossible pipe dreams. Even personal growth is not our god. We learn to accept limits. We learn to be human. We learn to accept the gift of good enough, and focus on our task.

Being good enough through Christ changes our life's question. We no longer ask, "How can we do it all and do it all perfectly?" Instead we ask, "What are we to do? What is our task?"

5

The Certainty of God's Love

The religious leaders of Jesus' day worked hard to excel for God. They had 613 detailed commandments for living an excellent life. They debated at length which of these 613 was most important.

One day an expert in these laws asked Jesus which was greatest. Jesus answered, " 'Love the Lord your God with all your heart and with all your soul and with all your mind.' This is the first and greatest commandment. And the second is like it: 'Love your neighbor as yourself.' "

What is our task? Jesus answers simply, "Love God and your neighbor."

The *Westminster Larger Catechism* phrases our task differently. It begins with the question: What is the chief end of man? It answers: Man's chief end is to glorify God and to enjoy him forever.

To love God and our neighbor. To glorify God and to enjoy him forever.

These answers provide a crucial context for finding our individual tasks in God's world. To understand *my* task, I need first to understand *our* task.

"Those are nice words," you say, "but what do they mean? I think I know what love is, but in day-to-day life, what does it mean to glorify God and enjoy him?"

In the Bible, the words translated *glory* (*kabod* and *doxa*) mean the presence of God dwelling in the midst of his people. We glorify God when we uncover or reveal his presence.

When God created the world, he chose to live in a relationship with it. He could have, I suppose, created it and flung it off somewhere to be a self-contained unit, but he didn't. He is continually present with us, and wants us to keep his will (his law) so the world will keep working properly.

When we live in the world as he intended it, we glorify him. When we bring the fallen world a step closer to the way he created it, we glorify him. When we develop and uncover more of its created possibilities, we glorify him.

In concrete terms, what does this mean? When we keep our houses and offices, our cities and parks, orderly instead of chaotic, we glorify God—because he is a God of order. When we are kind to the grumpy clerk and smile at him, we glorify God. We glorify God when we ground our teenager for violating a curfew, and when we prepare a birthday party.

We glorify him when we design windows which are more energy-efficient. We do it when we stock our store with items a community needs, when we type a letter at the office, when we fix the car, and when we launder clothes.

When Jesus told us to love our neighbor as ourself, he was telling us how to glorify God. We sometimes think of love as sentimentality, or perhaps a warm feeling, but it is more. Yes, love is feelings and warmth, but at its root love is care for the well-being of others. We love when we bring a pot of soup to a sick acquaintance. We love when we listen to a friend pour out her marriage problems. We love when we donate money for starving children.

Each slot we fill in life that helps meet a need is a way of loving, of providing for the welfare of our neighbor. The birthday parties, curfews, windows, typing, and laundering are also forms of love. To love your neighbor and to glorify God have the same essence.

But life is more than work! The Westminster catechism says the task is to glorify God *and enjoy him forever*. We are not only to love our neighbor, but to *love God above all*. Life is work *and worship*.

We follow God's pattern for living when we enjoy him forever, when we worship him. We worship God when we sing a hymn of joy in church—or in the shower. We worship God when we thank him for his love, when we praise him for who he is and how he has made us. We worship God when we revel in his Word.

We also enjoy God when we revel in his world. We revel in his revel-ation! We enjoy God when we stand transfixed under a rainbow. We enjoy God when we tickle our toddler's chin. We enjoy him when we breakfast on a brisk morning at a mountain campground. When we rejoice in what God has made, we also enjoy him.

In this, too, we follow his pattern. When God created the world he interspersed his work of creating with moments when he said, "It's good." When God had finished creating he rested. He leaned back in his celestial recliner, took a deep breath, and enjoyed the work of his hands. He took an entire day for enjoyment.

Was God tired? I don't think so. He wasn't resting to restore energy for more work. He was resting to enjoy his world. The same is true of our enjoyment of him. Worship fulfills its own end as worship. We don't worship just to work harder.

Josef Pieper said in *Leisure, the Basis of Culture*, that worship stands at right angles to work, totally different from it. It is existence in an extra dimension. It is the difference between dissecting a butterfly and watching its flight. It is the difference between helping your son with spelling and hugging him.

Do you watch the butterfly in order to dissect it? Do we

hug our children in order to improve their spelling? Of course not. Work is not the purpose of worship.

When excellence is our goal and achievement is the measure of worth, worship loses its meaning. We either worship in order to work, or we turn worship into work. Worship serves work when we have morning devotions because we find it increases our productivity. Worship becomes work when we attend church and pray only because they are our duties.

When in our drive for excellence worship serves work or becomes work, the double nature of our calling is blurred. Celebration of God's presence disappears. Joy vanishes. Joy becomes work when we celebrate a birthday simply to raise our son's self-esteem. Celebration is the servant of work when we go on vacations just to renew our energy for the job. Worship serves work when we sing hymns simply to improve our singing skills.

The double task for which we human beings are good enough is the task of glorifying God and enjoying him forever. It is the calling of work and worship. It is the task of loving our neighbor as ourselves and God above all.

God guarantees that this collective purpose for the body of believers will be accomplished. He will have his way with the world. He will be glorified and enjoyed. If we do not do it, the stones themselves will cry out, Jesus tells us in a hyperbole for the guarantee of God's fulfilled purpose in both time and eternity.

Within this larger context, each of us has tasks suited to our time and space. Adam and Eve were not called to invent a computer! We are all part of the same work crew, the same family. We are servant sons and daughters. We are God's hands in God's world, and each set of hands is promised the skills for its task. We are promised adequacy for our small corner of glorifying and enjoying God. And his grace promises that we will do that forever!

Even when our work seems to fail, we can remember his

promise, "in all things God works for the good of those who love him, who have been called according to his purpose."

What about the times, though, when we refuse to be called according to his purpose? What about the times we want to play God and do it all? For such proud rebellion, God's guarantee has also another face: forgiveness. When we treat others as ladder rungs for our climb, there is forgiveness. When we tell God what he owes us because we've worked so hard, there is forgiveness. When we feel self-sufficient and independent of him, he forgives.

Whenever we disobey his law, his will for our lives, he is willing to forgive. Because of Christ, all we need to do is ask. When we return, he's at the door welcoming us returning prodigals with open arms.

With the guarantees of adequacy and forgiveness, God runs an apparent risk. If we are promised adequacy and forgiveness, why try? Why not just lie down and sleep? God doesn't need our work, and he'll cover us with his grace anyway.

No, said theologian Neal Plantinga. That's like saying the fire department gives us permission to set fires, or that a lifeguard on duty permits us to swim out beyond our range. Grace is not permission to sin. Paul makes that clear in Romans 6. "Shall we go on sinning so that grace may increase? By no means!"

We are called to glorify and enjoy God. We good-enough people are still called to God's service, because that is how he chooses to work his way. Plantinga reminds us of the price Jesus paid: "Grace may be free, but it is not cheap. It always comes to us with blood on it." Bought at such a price, it's unthinkable to be lazy. Bought at such a price, it's folly to rebel.

Although the guarantees of grace are not designed to produce laziness or rebellion, they can promote for us a sense of distance from our work. With these promises, we no longer identify so closely with it. The founder of the Jesuits experienced that distance when he said that if his entire life's work collapsed, he would mourn for half an hour and then go on with his life. That's distance!

We cannot always see how our lives fit God's larger purposes. By God's grace Corrie Ten Boom's disastrous life in a concentration camp became a springboard for her ministry to millions.

How do we treat our apparent successes and disasters? In his poem "If" Rudyard Kipling described adulthood as an ability to "meet with triumph and disaster and treat those two imposters just the same." To treat the two imposters the same is to have distance. We simply go about our work and our worship, not asking the question of quality.

After World War II, when Dutch Christians who had risked their lives hiding Jews from the Gestapo were asked about their decision, they didn't consider themselves heroes. "What choice did we have?" they asked. "We simply did what we had to do." They did the task before them, not asking any achievement questions.

When we have distance, we are enabled to recognize some disappointments as our misunderstanding of our task. You may think your task is to raise a prodigy, and discover your son has learning disabilities. You may think you are called to a teaching position, and learn that the contract has been given to someone else.

C. S. Lewis creates a marvelous picture of a changing understanding of God's will in his science fiction fantasy *Perelandra*. Perelandra is a perfect world with a golden sky and exotic fruits to which the scientist Ransom is sent from fallen earth.

When Perelandra's sinless Eve searches for her husband and finds Ransom instead, he asks her if she is disappointed. It takes her a moment to understand him, and then, after comparing it to finding a different fruit from the one she was seeking, she says:

But this I had never noticed before—that the very moment of finding there is in the mind a kind of thrusting back, or setting aside. The picture of the fruit you have *not* found is still, for a moment, before you. And if you wished—if it were possible to wish—you could keep it there. You could send your soul after the good you had expected, instead of turning it to the good you had got. You could refuse the real good; you could make the real fruit taste insipid by thinking of the other.

In our fallen world it's not quite so simple, because good is not all that happens. The forces of evil are also at work. But, it is a world both fallen and redeemed. We have the guarantee: despite evil, God will be glorified and worshiped. And all things, including the evil, can work to good for those who love him and are called according to his purpose.

He tells us finite children in this imperfect world, "My grace is sufficient for you." He tells us his strength is made perfect in our weakness.

These promises, too, can give us that distance. They can free us from the roller coaster of identifying too closely with our work. They exchange the burden of excellence for the burden of love, the burden of glorifying and enjoying him. That yoke is easy and that burden is light. It is a hiking path through a woods, not a marathon race to be first to the finish line.

Bearing God's burden, living by his will, is simply life as he created it to be. In seeking the tasks he assigns lies freedom. A goldfish living in an aquarium is free to live as a fish. If we give it the freedom of the whole living room by placing it on the carpet, it gasps and dies. When we make excellence our measure, we turn ourselves into goldfish on the carpet. When we love, when we glorify and enjoy God, we are free to swim in his marvelous aquarium. In fact, it's not an aquarium but an entire ocean of love.

The choice between the carpet and the ocean is the choice between excellence and good enough.

Let's stop a moment and follow the thread of the past five chapters. We've seen that voices cry for excellence, both within us and around us. We've seen that the word *excellence* is powerful, but filled with contradictory meanings. Even if we select a noncontradictory meaning, we find ourselves with an insatiable drive to earn worth, either by being God, or by trying to deserve his love. We've seen that worth is a gift of being loved by God through Christ, and through that love we are good enough, good enough for the tasks of glorifying and worshiping him.

When I weigh the alternatives, I find that good enough is better than excellent. For me and my life, I'll accept the gift of good enough. How about you?

Are you with me in choosing this option? If so, you face two challenges. The first is to remain aware that you are "good enough." The second challenge is to find your own personal tasks within God's world. That's examined in the final five chapters.

Facing those two challenges can fill your life with joy, for the gift of good enough is a gift wrapped in joy.

The tools in the next seven chapters are for staying awake to God's gift of good enough. But they are dangerous tools, because they can be wrongly used as whips, goads, or prods. You can say to yourself, "If I were really a good Christian, I should use these tools perfectly. I should feel good enough all the time, and I should never feel driven to excellence."

If you do that, do you see what you've done? You've set up a new achievement ethic: I must always feel good enough.

Not true! God does not require such feelings.

Use the following chapters as optional tools, not whips. They aren't prods to produce guilt, but erasers to help eliminate it! Use those which help you accept your gift of being good enough. Discard those which don't.

6

Challenging Your Shoulds

At 13 I sewed half a dozen bean bags for my younger brothers. They rated the bags top-notch. I then hemmed dish towels for my mother. Another success.

I decided I was ready to sew myself a dress—a simple shift pattern with straight lines, long sleeves, and a small collar.

I cut the pattern pieces handily and read the instructions. They said to sew with a ⅝-inch seam allowance.

"Whatever for?" I wondered. "I sew straight seams. I won't go off the edge. I should be able to sew on just a ¼-inch seam allowance with no problem."

I blithely sewed front and back together on beautifully straight ¼-inch seams. But, no matter how I tugged and stretched, I couldn't get the sleeves and collar to fit. Why? Because I was sewing on a ¼-inch seam!

I had tried to improve on the pattern. I had misunderstood the purpose of the ⅝-inch seam and tried to live by a "higher" standard. I had created my own "should."

I am still sewing on a ¼-inch seam when I think my marriage should be continuous romance. When I think my children should never fight, I'm sewing on a ¼-inch seam. When I think I need to win a tennis match to feel good about it, I am sewing on a ¼-inch seam.

Many of the shoulds we carry around with us are improper standards that don't fit God's pattern for our lives. Our shoulds sometimes are more demanding than his. We sew on ¼-inch seams and then can't figure out why the pieces of our lives don't fit into a 24-hour day. When we take on more tasks than time allows, when we are dissatisfied with less than total recall, when we wish we had smaller noses—we aren't following God's pattern for life. We're trying to make our own rules for fitting the pieces together.

We do the same when we say people who love each other should never disagree, or believe we should never be angry.

The word *should* is rooted in an Anglo-Saxon word for scold, and that's exactly what our shoulds do. Our shoulds are often ugly, scolding voices that choke joy. They are taskmasters who overflow with criticism and run dry on praise.

When we don't live up to our list of shoulds, we punish ourselves with "should haves." The shoulds create pressure and tension. The should haves create guilt and depression.

Ruth is a young farmwife with four children who works full time as a secretary. "I feel as if there are more things I should be doing," she says. "For example, I always feel as if I really should learn to sew, that every worthwhile mother should sew clothes for her kids and curtains for her windows."

Ruth doesn't sew, but she does do the minor electrical and mechanical repairs around the house. However, her secretarial job and her home repairs don't deter the scolding voice inside. She still feels she should be learning to sew.

Gloria has a different should. When I stepped into her immaculate living room for a committee meeting, she directed me to put my coat in the first room on the right. I missed the first door and had my hand on the knob of the second when she quickly redirected me to the first. "No one is allowed beyond that door," she said with a nervous laugh. "I haven't

cleaned my bedroom." Her voice was tense, her face flushed.
Gloria had violated her should for housekeeping.

She confessed, "It's embarrassing. I feel as if my house
should always be in perfect order, but it isn't. I'm so often
called to a meeting and go off with the dishes sitting on the
counter or an unmade bed."

Seated across the room, Beth felt the pressure of a different
should. "I simply can't leave the house when it's messy," she
said. "I admire people who can. I feel I should be able to, but
I can't."

Beth and Gloria feel pressure from shoulds which are exact
opposites. And they feel ashamed of violating those shoulds.

We all function with long lists of shoulds. Some of those
shoulds are legitimate. I should feed my children. I should get
some rest at night. I should dress warmly in winter weather.

But, in Pharisee fashion, we pile should upon should. I
should always feel warmth toward my spouse. I should always
know the answer to my children's questions. I should be able
to begin a job away from home, and still maintain my current
activities.

Psychologist Aaron Beck, in *Cognitive Therapy and the
Emotional Disorders,* lists the following typical unrealistic
shoulds:

1. I should be the utmost of generosity, considerateness, dignity, courage, unselfishness.
2. I should be the perfect lover, friend, parent, teacher, student, spouse.
3. I should be able to endure any hardship with equanimity.
4. I should be able to find a quick solution to every problem.
5. I should never feel hurt; I should always be happy and
   serene.
6. I should know, understand, and foresee everything.
7. I should always be spontaneous; I should always control
   my feelings.
8. I should assert myself; I should never hurt anybody else.

9. I should never be tired or get sick.
10. I should always be at peak efficiency.

We live with all kinds of shoulds—ridiculous shoulds, wrong-purpose shoulds, false-responsibility shoulds, outdated shoulds, and vague shoulds.

Ridiculous shoulds

Three years ago, after having dabbled in it occasionally, Judy took her first-ever local tennis clinic. The instructor walked members of the tennis club through the proper footwork and arm motions for ground strokes and volleys. Because that was new material for Judy, she needed the instructions repeated. As the other members of the club handily stroked balls over the net, the instructor walked her through the motions again. She felt tense, embarrassed, pressured.

Why? Judy said, "After I thought it through, I realized that I felt I should be able to master the motions easily, retaining them perfectly on a single pass, even though I know that muscle training takes repetition." Judy was listening to an unreasonable, ridiculous should.

Wrong-purpose shoulds

Before Karen's relatives came for a weekend, she spent two days grouchy and pressured, trying to get her house in perfect order. She yelled at her children for spilling milk. She told them to clean their closets and polish their shoes. She mopped the kitchen floor and moved the living room furniture to vacuum under it. She even reorganized the boxes in the storage room.

She baked banana bread and cookies, swept the garage, and trimmed the shrubs. Her should was: have the house and yard in perfect order when the relatives arrive. Why? To impress them with her housekeeping skills, and to be sure they couldn't fault her as a homemaker. What kind of a purpose was that? Wasn't the real purpose of her home to provide a comfortable environment for fellowship? Her you-should-clean-house-to-impress-the-relatives was a wrong-purpose should.

False-responsibility shoulds

Two of my sons began their morning with a disagreement. They continued bickering through breakfast. I asked them to stop. They kept on. I separated them at opposite ends of the table. They began to call each other names. I called for silence. They stuck out their tongues at each other. I gave them cereal boxes to use as barriers so they couldn't see each other.

They finished breakfast and headed for the school bus jostling each other for lead position.

I sat down with a cup of tea and moaned my failure as a mother. "Brothers should get along," I thought. "I should be able to halt their squabbles. I should be able to control them."

I used the should of false responsibility, forgetting that they also made choices and had some responsibility for their own behavior.

The should of false responsibility might be operating when a leader feels totally responsible for a stimulating group discussion. Certainly Dottie felt it when she wrote in her annual Christmas letter, "Jim is so busy at work and so pressured that it takes all of my energy just to keep him going."

Outdated shoulds

Each spring Thelma felt compelled to wash the walls in her home from top to bottom. Some springs she heeded the urge. Sometimes she washed only the bottom, where her youngsters' fingerprints showed. When she washed only half, she felt guilty. Her mother had always washed the whole wall. So had her grandmother.

One summer, she was surprised to hear her mother say, "It was a blessing to not wash my walls this spring. Now that we got rid of that coal furnace there's no soot buildup over the winter." Thelma had been hearing an outdated should.

Some of our other domestic shoulds may also be scrubbing nonexistent soot. When we feel pressure to keep a garden and preserve summer produce, we may be hearing the echoes of an outdated should. For our grandmothers those duties were essential for survival. We have a choice.

Vague shoulds

One day last summer I had my three sons home and was baby-sitting three additional children. Two were outside in the sandbox, two were in the family room pulling toys from the toy cupboard, and the third pair was finishing snacks in the kitchen. Each pair had an attention span of about five minutes before moving on to a new activity. I settled squabbles, wiped noses, provided sandbox toys, and refilled juice glasses, picking up clutter as I moved from child to child. I kept thinking, "I'm not getting anything done. I should be doing something more." But I had no clear idea of what that something more was.

Many of our shoulds can be simply vague, free-floating thoughts.

Challenging your shoulds

What can we do about these shoulds? Do we let them rule and ruin our lives? Do we bow meekly to their scolding tyranny? No. We challenge them. We question their right to rule over us.

Often the process of challenging a should lies in first discovering what that should is. All of our shoulds—the ridiculous, the wrong purpose, the false responsibility, the outdated, and the vague—may simply be unarticulated feelings. We need a process to bring those shoulds to light.

Aaron Beck calls this process "tapping internal communications." Between an external event and an emotional response, he says, lies an "automatic thought," of which we are almost unaware. An automatic thought gives meaning to the external event. When your preschooler starts to cry in the grocery store and strangers glance your way with disapproval, you may wish you could instantly vanish. Why do you wish that? You may think it is your child's tantrum which causes your embarrassment. In fact, it may be your hidden standard: "Strangers should always approve of me."

When you turn down a request that you serve on the church music committee and feel guilty, you may think your guilt comes simply from saying no. But, underlying that guilt may be a should: I should never turn down a request from a worthwhile project.

Because such thoughts are automatic, we are scarcely aware of them, and it does not occur to us to question them. Of course strangers should approve of us. Of course we should say yes to worthwhile volunteer work. We see our shoulds as unquestionable law.

For those of us driven to excellence those automatic thoughts are often achievement oriented: I should be the best at _____ . I should be a top-notch _____ . I should improve at _____ .

To challenge those thoughts, you first need to bring them to a conscious level. How do you do that? To unearth the hidden shoulds I have found journal-keeping a useful tool.

When I find myself caught by depression or guilt, I take the next free moments in my day to write my way through my feelings. I start by writing what happened. I then pour out how I'm feeling about it. I ask myself what automatic thought or hidden should is causing the feeling. What standard am I violating? I remind myself that events don't cause my feelings; my interpretation of the event causes my feelings. Having found the hidden should, I challenge it. Is it realistic? Is it serving a good purpose? Am I making myself totally responsible? In the final step, I challenge the automatic thought. Sometimes I decide my should is valid. Often, however, I find it is not.

This journal process, in a nutshell, includes four steps:

1. Name the event.
2. State your feeling about that event.
3. Identify the automatic thought or should which causes the feeling. (Remember, the event doesn't cause the negative feeling. Your interpretation of the event does.)
4. Challenge the should or automatic thought. You need to check your perception against reality. Not all shoulds need to be discarded—just the ones which don't match reality.

Let's walk through an example of the process.

Your friend Marie has just sung a marvelous solo in a December performance of the Messiah. She's in the foyer surrounded by admirers and well-wishers. You feel jealous, guilty, blue. Your voice quavered a trifle off-key during congregational singing.

Event: Marie sang a beautiful solo.

Feelings: Envy. Jealousy. Guilt.

Possible hidden shoulds: I should be a better singer. I should develop my voice. I should always be the center of attention.

Challenges: I am a finite, limited human being. I am not God. Performance singing is not a gift I am called to develop. I do not always need to be the center of attention to have worth. (You can use a similar challenge when an acquaintance displays a handmade quilt, completes a master's degree, or begins foster parenting.)

You will find in writing your journal that the process isn't quite as short and straightforward as the above summaries. You may have to write your way through an outpouring of anger, depression, guilt, frustration, before you can see clearly to the underlying issues. Just let the words and feelings flow. After all the emotion has poured over the dam, you will find a peaceful pool into which you can peer for shoulds beneath the surface.

After I had been using my journal for several months, I found that after the outpouring of feeling I could hear another voice other than the voice of my anger, my guilt, my shoulds. I could hear a still, small voice of reality—a sensible voice, a questioning voice. I named this voice within me "the friendly therapist" and entered her responses in my journal as well. To give that voice more power, I found myself emphasizing my friendly therapist voice.

A section of my journal from the day I was caring for six children and feeling I should accomplish more, reads:
I'm not getting anything done. I really should be getting something done. I'm so frustrated because I'm just not getting anywhere today.
What is it that you should be doing differently?
I don't know, just something else, something more.
What?
I'm not sure. I just never get enough done. There are never enough hours in the day.
Really! There are never enough hours to get done what you want, but you don't know what it is you want to get done.
I didn't really think of it that way.
And that "never" is a pretty sweeping generalization for one morning of baby-sitting, isn't it?
I guess so.
Do you consider caring for six youngsters nothing?
Well, no, I guess it is something.
If you don't know what it is you should be doing differently, perhaps you can give yourself permission to do the tasks you see until that becomes clear to you.
Perhaps I can.

Sometimes the voice of the friendly therapist uncovers the hidden should. The day my sons persisted fighting, my journal (after the outpouring of frustration) read:
I am frustrated and nothing I try seems to stop the fighting and teasing and nagging. I feel like a failure.
Why do you feel like a failure?
Because they didn't stop fighting.
So boys should never fight.

I guess all children fight sometimes, but I should be able to stop them.

You should always be able to stop their fighting. You have total control over their behavior?

No, I guess they do make some choices in their lives now that they are grade schoolers.

So what is your responsibility?

To set up a calm and ordered atmosphere, to penalize fighting beyond a certain limit, and let them choose between the penalty and stopping fighting, I guess.

So what was the automatic thought that was causing you to feel like a failure?

I guess my standard that brothers should never fight and that I am totally responsible for their behavior.

Is that an accurate view of the world or a workable standard?

No, I guess it isn't.

So what's out of whack, the should or the behavior?

The should.

Right! Good for you!

The goal of putting things on paper, whatever form that takes for you, is to clarify your thinking. The process forces you to concentrate on the issues. When psychotherapist Cal Meuzelaar suggests clients try writing to clarify their thinking he tells them, "You don't have to be an author. I'm not interested in smooth writing or complete sentences. It doesn't even have to be spelled right. I just want you to get your thoughts down. Get them down on paper."

Cal comments that they sometimes come back with fragments scribbled on torn pieces of paper. "They apologize, and I tell them it's OK. Then we get to work, reading through those scribbled thoughts," he said. They begin examining the client's yardsticks for life.

It was a landmark day in my life when I began to discover that sometimes when I didn't measure up, it was my yardstick and not my life that was at fault.

For some, though, that voice of the friendly therapist may

not be easy to activate alone. It may take the voice of a real
therapist to get you started, to tell you, "It doesn't even have
to be spelled right—just get it down!" Or it may take the voice
of a good friend in whom you can confide. Choose a good
friend who will tell it to you straight, who will level with you
when she hears you setting unrealistic standards, setting up
ridiculous shoulds, not giving yourself permission to be finite,
to be human.

Close friends can help you shrink your yardstick. I meet
regularly with two small groups: a group of writers and a group
of mothers. In both groups I find resources to help me see my
parenting and my writing more clearly. I find fuel to challenge
my shoulds.

Once you have had practice in identifying your shoulds,
you may be able sometimes to shorten the process. Sometimes
you may be able to think it through without resorting to your
journal. Whether you follow this process in your head or on
paper, it is never over. Each stage of life reveals to us more
shoulds to be examined, more automatic thoughts to be tested
against reality.

We excellence seekers live with lots of untested shoulds—
and often with a gigantic shouldn't. Before you turn the page
take 10 seconds to guess what it is. OK, time is up. Give up?
If you haven't got the answer, how do you feel about that?
Frustrated? Defeated? Are you responding to a should that
says: "Always know the answers"? Is that a realistic should?
Take a moment to sort that through using the processes of this
chapter before moving on.

7

Challenging Your Shouldn'ts

After I finished graduate school, the employment agency through which I sought work offered me a job as one of its employment counselors. I accepted, and was immediately confronted with masses of information to absorb—job openings, employers, companies, job types, and applicant qualifications. I had to master telephone sales skills and personal interview skills.

I gave 101% to the task—asking lots of questions, imitating my fellow counselors' techniques, and memorizing mountains of data. After a month on the job, I was proud of the speed of my mastery of new skills. I also was tense, tired, and had acid indigestion—but I was pleased with myself.

A half year later, the supervisor of the agency said to me over lunch, "You know, we were all worried about you the first couple of months. You just didn't give yourself permission to make a mistake."

While I had been proudly mastering the job, my colleagues had been concerned about my perfectionism!

What is your reaction to making mistakes? For some people, the drive for excellence is not so much a list of shoulds as one gigantic shouldn't: I shouldn't make mistakes.

When a young psychotherapist was ready to begin his first job as a counselor, he was worried. "What if I make a mistake?" he asked his supervising psychiatrist.

The psychiatrist answered, "Oh, you don't need to worry about that. You *will* make a mistake. Not only that, but you will make a second mistake—and then another, and another, and another. And after that you will make yet another mistake. But that's OK."

Mistakes.

We all make them.

We dislike making them.

For some of us that dislike becomes the driving force of perfectionism. This gigantic shouldn't can produce effects similar to those of the shoulds: workaholism, tension, and depression. But it can also produce other effects.

Mark said, "My perfectionism causes me daily grief. I'm not willing to try something unless I know it can be perfect. It keeps me from producing in ways I really could, but don't." Fear of mistakes narrows his life.

Dorothy said, "I put off doing things until I can do them perfectly. The projects just pile up. The mending waits until my kids have outgrown the jeans, because I wait until I have time to make perfect patches. My hutch is in the basement awaiting varnishing. The window trim still needs a final coat of paint. Last fall, the pressure of these projects finally gave me the beginning of an ulcer." Dorothy's big "shouldn't" resulted in procrastination.

Procrastinating people may actually be defeated perfectionists. They can't be mistake-free and so they don't try. They give up because they can't measure up. Instead of changing their unreasonable standards, they give up on their lives, either by shrinking them or putting off tasks.

What they don't realize, however, is that narrow and procrastinating perfectionism is one of the biggest mistakes of all! *We don't learn if we don't make mistakes. We don't grow.* If you define *excellence* as not making a mistake, you have lopped off an entire creative world. The need to explore a hundred blind alleys before finding the open road is fundamental to creativity. It requires trial and error. For every page appearing in this book, I have created five or ten that have been discarded. For every polished piano solo my husband performs, he has played that music dozens of times with wrong notes and less satisfying interpretations.

Thomas Edison had many failures before he created a working light bulb. Eve and Pierre Curie explored many blind alleys before isolating polonium and radium for which they were awarded a 1903 Nobel Prize.

Did your toddler take her first step with perfect balance? First she fell. Did your two-year-old pronounce his first word without error? Of course not. When he said, "Da-da" did you correct him? Did you say, "No, honey, that's wrong. It's not da-da, it's daddy." Of course you didn't.

We who fear failure ask the same silly question my husband tells me I asked while talking in my sleep. "I've never done this before," I said. "Are you sure I'm getting it right?" If you've never done it before, you can be sure you're *not* doing it right—but that's OK. That's exploration. That's creativity. That's growth. That's part of the image of God!

Our fear of mistakes can be distorted thinking, paralyzing and narrowing us. That fear is sometimes based on distorted logic in which we make a hasty—and incorrect—generalization. That generalization can take several forms.

"One mistake means failure." This thinking sets the world up into two camps: heroes and villains, superwomen and dumpy frumps, successes and failures. With these standards, if you don't get straight A's, you've failed the course. If you eat a piece of cheesecake during your diet, you have totally blown it. If you skip jogging for a weekend, you are a physical flop.

But such thinking is distorted. One piece of cheesecake will ruin your diet only if you decide it will. And B's are also respectable grades. They mean, after all, you mastered 80-90% of the material!

"This failure is going to be repeated over and over." When Sesame Street's muppet composer is told by Kermit that two words in his song don't rhyme, he often collapses over the piano, bongs his head on the keys, and moans, "Oh, I'll never get it right. Never, never, never!"

That's distorted thinking! David Burns calls this kind of prediction a fortune teller error, a sort of self-fulfilling prophecy.

The muppet has human counterparts, however. We laugh at his frustration, his head-bonging, and his prediction, because we see in them a caricature of ourselves.

We forget a friend's birthday and we say, "I can never remember it." But such predictions are distortions. They need not be true. My being late for work today does not mean I will automatically be late tomorrow. My dialing a telephone number incorrectly once doesn't mean it will happen again and again.

Our mistake does not cause us to be trapped forever, but our prediction may. Our prediction may become a sort of self-fulfilling prophecy. We think we will repeat the mistake; therefore we do.

"I have always made this mistake." When I rubbed my eye and dislodged a gray contact lens, which fell to the gray cement and mingled invisibly with the popcorn and candy wrappers at an outdoor concert, I was upset. "Why do I always lose things?" I berated myself.

It was the first contact lens I had lost in 10 years! But at that moment, I did not allow myself to retrieve that information. I wanted to punish myself with, "I always lose things."

When we make a mistake, we sometimes turn on a memory filter which allows us to make negative generalizations. "I never remember names," we say. But we do remember the names of our children, our spouse, our parents, our friends. We only forget sometimes—and that's usually when we're under pressure. Our negative filter darkens our past.

To challenge the big shouldn't and its distorted thinking, you can use some of the same techniques you use for challenging your shoulds. You can write an event on paper, using your journal. You can activate the voice of the friendly therapist to uncover some of your distorted thinking and challenge it.

I used the voice of the friendly therapist the night I drove to an origami class and discovered I'd written the class on my calendar for the wrong night.

Our conversation went something like this:

I hate it. I hate making dumb mistakes like this. I always make dumb mistakes.

What actually happened?

I wrote down the wrong date and missed the origami class.

Did you really miss it? The actual class is tomorrow night, isn't it? You can go then, can't you?

Yes, I suppose. But I'm always getting glitches like that.

Really? When was your last glitch?

Well, there was the wedding I went to an hour early and the time I forgot I was supposed to babysit for Doug and the time I forgot to work in the church nursery. . . .

Over what time span? When was the wedding?

Well . . . That was 10 years ago.

Ten years ago. Do your examples really add up to always making dumb mistakes?

No, I guess not.

And can you tell me what harm is done by this mistake?

Well, I lost half an hour of time coming and going.

Anything else?

No, but I'm upset that I did it.

Why?

Because I shouldn't make mistakes like that.

You don't have the right to make mistakes, not even occasional ones with no serious harm done?

Well, yes, I guess I do.

The voice of the friendly therapist can help you uncover the big shouldn't: I shouldn't make mistakes.

It can also help you identify your distorted thinking. I used the friendly therapist the day I opened the clothes hamper to discover that my husband's new, white tennis shirt had sprouted mildew.

You are feeling like a failure.

Yes.

Exactly what happened?

What happened? What happened? I let Marlo's new shirt grow mountains of mildew when I should have laundered it. I'll never make a good housekeeper. I just can't stay organized enough.

Oh, you should have laundered the shirt sooner?

Yes.

You've been sitting around eating too many chocolate bonbons this week?

No—there were special activities at church and the kids' swimming lessons, and the summer tutoring, and . . .

You made other choices?

Yes.

What did you say a few sentences back about the future?

I'll never be a good housekeeper.

I see. You intend to keep repeating this mistake?

No, I don't intend to, but it could happen.

Is that prediction necessarily accurate?

No, I guess not.

And does one mildewed shirt wipe out all of the other housekeeping you've done this year?

No.

Do you see how you were falling into a trap of all-or-nothing thinking?

Yes, I see.

In a shorter version of writing things out, you can simply describe the event on paper and write how you feel about it.

Then read through what you've written. Are you thinking you shouldn't make mistakes? Are you thinking that this mistake makes you a total failure? That it will be repeated? That you always make this mistake? Find your distorted thinking and challenge it!

Talking through the big shouldn't with friends may help, too. When a friend says she was up until midnight trying to track down the missing penny in her checkbook balance, I see her as a mirror of myself.

A writer friend recently made a decision about a book manuscript, saying, "I'm just going to go ahead and finish it. I know it's not going to be the final word on the subject. People will criticize it. But I'm just going to go ahead with it and offer it as my little gift to my world." When she said that, I found a model which freed me to continue offering my gift as well.

One technique that also removes the power of the big shouldn't is to rename your mistakes. Don't call them mistakes: call them opportunities to learn. Then ask yourself what you can learn from them. From the missed origami class I learned that when I rush I work less accurately. From the mildewed shirt I learned that scheduling laundry more frequently in the summer might be a good idea.

Robert Raines writes in *Success Is a Moving Target,* "Nothing succeeds like failure. We learn far more about ourselves in our failures than in our successes." Use your mistakes as stepping stones to cross life's river, not as whips for bloodying your back.

Another way to challenge your attitude toward imperfection is to set up a perfection time block. Try just half an hour in which you will consciously try to do everything perfectly. Ready? Begin! Are you now sitting with perfect posture? Gracefully rise from your chair, go to your kitchen, and make yourself a glass of juice from that frozen concentrate in your refrigerator. Did you retain your grip on the little plastic pull-tab on the first try? Did you get every last drop of the concentrate from the can? Did you add exactly the right amount of water—not one drop too much? Was your stirring motion the most efficient one possible for dissolving the concentrate?

You say you want to quit? I'm sorry, only four minutes of your half hour have elapsed. Please continue on your own for 26 minutes (not one second more or less), choosing your own activities.

At the end of the time, take half an hour in which you give yourself conscious permission to do things imperfectly. At the end of that time, ask yourself which half hour you enjoyed more. Then choose to live imperfectly with joy!

Do you know of anyone who doesn't make mistakes? Do you think Jesus made mistakes? (Do you really think he spoke perfect Aramaic at birth?) A mistake is not a sin. Examine the restrictions that come from your fear of mistakes. Look at what happens to your mood when you don't give yourself permission to err. Look at your own attitude toward people who are terrified of mistakes. Are you comfortable around them?

Living with our family as I write this is Nhung Nguyen, an 18-year-old Vietnamese Christian three years away from Vietnam. Our role is to provide her a Christian environment for this school year and to speed her transition into American culture.

Someday a study by eminent sociologists may declare: The transplanting of Vietnamese adolescents into American homes produced long-term identity confusion. I don't know about that, but I am willing to run the risk. I am learning, in Luther's phrase, to "sin boldly" rather than being paralyzed for fear of doing something wrong. I am learning to make mistakes.

8

Forgiven, Not Driven

At 15 I wanted to be a flight attendant, complete with svelte clothes and false eyelashes. I imagined myself flitting the skies from city to sophisticated city, looking glamorous during the days and spending glorious evenings at theatres and concerts coast-to-coast.

An airlines brochure explained the miraculous makeup sessions that were part of the training, and I decided I might be able to fix my face. I read eagerly about the classes teaching how to move with grace and ease. I pictured my lanky frame transformed.

Then, in the small print, I found the height requirement. Maximum height allowed was 5'9".

My dreams collapsed. No makeup or movement classes could trim three inches from my six-foot frame. I was barred from the ranks of glamorous flight attendants forever. I would never be short enough to qualify.

I felt humiliated. By being too tall, I did not measure up. I was angry with myself and God. I felt worthless. I felt inadequate. I wasn't physically good enough to meet the standards for flight attendants.

When I fly today, I see another side of attending flights.

I see hard work in cramped quarters under tight deadlines. But in my dreamy-eyed adolescence I saw only the glamour. Stewardesses—as we called them then—were ideals, heroines for me and for half a dozen of my classmates.

When I failed to measure up to that ideal, I experienced shame. My dictionary tells me that the painful emotion of shame I experience can be caused by awareness of three kinds of failings: 1) impropriety, 2) shortcoming, or 3) guilt.

Those three failings are different. Impropriety is to violate some standard of society, some social convention. When I burp in public or shout at a formal concert, I have been improper. When I eat spaghetti with my fingers, I commit an impropriety. To avoid impropriety, I must know the customs of a culture (or subculture) and conform to those customs.

A shortcoming is to fall short of some ideal, some hero. If our ideal has an IQ of above 130, we feel our children fall short when they test out at 95. If our heroine wears a size 10, we experience shortcoming when we're a plump size 14.

Finally, guilt is a failure to measure up in the eyes of the law. If I ride through a red light, I have violated a law. If I fail to report all of my income, I am guilty of violating the law.

To use the term of the previous chapter, we experience shame for violating *shoulds* from three different sources. And sometimes we misname all three kinds of shame as guilt. We sometimes say we feel guilty when what we are really experiencing is shame and not guilt at all. Just as civil guilt results from violation of civil law, so moral guilt results from violation of God's moral law. To sin—to violate God's law—produces guilt. I have not measured up to that law.

But violating social conventions or being less than our hero is not sin! The only sin is violation of God's law. And the only real guilt is caused by that violation. My shame for improprieties or shortcomings is not guilt. That shame is not because of sin. It was no sin for me to be too tall for airline standards at 15. But I felt shame! I feel that same shame today when I accept advertising and movie industry standards for appearance and find myself wanting. I do the same today when I accept the standard of money, power, and prestige to judge my worth. I do the same today when I feel compelled to raise kids who are bright and attractive because that is the societal standard. I feel shame because of impropriety.

Sometimes I have internalized these values, incorporated them into my own heroine, and then I feel shame because I have violated my superself, the ideal me. The ideal me never runs out of energy, is always well-groomed, always has time to say yes to worthwhile volunteer work, is always organized, and never harried. The ideal me accomplishes mountains of work with a molehill of time. The ideal me never feels blue, not even with a premenstrual hormone imbalance. When I fall short of this heroine, I feel shame.

In both cases, we feel shame for violating false shoulds which we have already seen can be challenged.

But what about the real shoulds? Although most Christians I know load their backs with shoulds, it is possible to have too few shoulds. I remember a renegade fellow student saying to me, "There are only two things I *have* to do in life— die and pay taxes—and the taxes are optional."

That student wanted to erase all shoulds. But there are real shoulds! We don't live in a world without structure, a world without law. We need to separate the shoulds.

My husband and I should care for our children's needs. I should honor and love God and use his name with respect. I should obey authority and respect the lives and property rights of others. I should be content with where God has placed me and what he has given me. I should love God above all, and my neighbor as myself.

But often I try to live my own way. I am selfish. I put myself at the center of my life. I decide that a good end justifies my sidestepping the law. Or I succumb to temptation against my will. Sometimes I rebel against God's guidelines, even when I don't want to. As Paul says, "For what I do is not the good

I want to do; no, the evil I do not want to do—this I keep on doing."

When I know my true guilt before God, and experience shame, the solution is not to challenge the should. The solution to guilt-caused shame lies elsewhere. But the first step is to recognize the difference. "The aim of a healthy faith," says Alan McGinnis, "is to distinguish between false guilt [shame because of impropriety or shortcoming] and genuine guilt, then help a person expiate that guilt rather than wallow in it."

How do we expiate that guilt? For guilt-caused shame, we can't eliminate the should. The should is real! And we have violated it! But that shame doesn't have to live eternally in the human breast. The solution for that shame is confession. The solution for that shame is grace. The power of those real shoulds is wiped away by Christ.

Because of grace, even the should of God's law has no power to condemn us. It has no power to keep us in shame. Even before the law of God we have the gift of good enough.

"There is now no condemnation for those who are in Christ Jesus," the Bible tells us. Because of Christ's taking our condemnation, we are no longer condemned. We are forgiven! We are good enough forever.

Good enough people know their forgiveness is a gift unearned. Good enough people can accept the gift and live with joy. Good enough people can fail and still have joy. Good enough people care about their lives, but they don't carry the burden of the world on their shoulders (they know it's carried for them by the same shoulders that carried a cross). Good enough people don't compare themselves to others, but realize the varieties of gifts. Good enough people can return as prodigal children to the loving arms of their Father.

Good enough people need not feel guilt-caused shame for long. And it's not wise to allow the other kinds of shame to last too long or grow intense, because false shame can mask true guilt. It can set up a mist that hides us from the light of God. When we are busy being ashamed of how we look, of our lack of intelligence, of not being perfect, or making mistakes, we conceal our true guilt of not living in a right relationship with God. When we are busy being ashamed of aging, we don't notice that God has faded from our life. We use his name but not his power. Our false shame interferes with knowing our guilt and asking forgiveness.

Shame can interfere with experiencing the power of grace in our lives. When we are busy with shame over our children's fighting, we can forget to love them—to listen, look, hug, and touch. When Laura gave herself permission to stop feeling totally responsible for her children, when she stopped cringing in shame whenever they bickered, she made a discovery. She said, "After they'd been bickering one afternoon, I took my oldest son to a different room and told him, 'I love you very much and you are special to me. I haven't made that so clear lately, and I just wanted you to know how I feel.' Tears welled up in his eyes and he said, 'I don't always feel that way. I feel like Jim gets all the praise and all of the attention. You don't say good things about me very often.' What came out of my release from shame was a new openness with my son."

Shame for shortcoming or impropriety is not shame for sin. But there's a hidden twist to that kind of shame. Being too tall for the airline was no sin, but I was guilty of something entirely different. I was not guilty of wrong height, but I was guilty of a false standard. I was listening to a law other than God's. Sometimes when we feel this kind of shame, we are heeding a different law and serving a different god. We follow the law of social acceptability and serve the god of superself: infinite, all-knowing, all-powerful, perfect, super-me. I may need forgiveness, all right, not for my failure to measure up, but for my false standards.

We need forgiveness for thinking our true self is infinite. We need forgiveness for wanting to be superhuman, for wanting to be God. The prayer is not, "Lord forgive me for being tired and out of energy." Even Jesus got tired. The prayer is, "Lord forgive me for not accepting my human need for rest."

The prayer is not, "Lord, forgive me for forgetting Cheryl's name today," but "Lord, forgive me for thinking I should have total recall."

Trying to evade shame by singleminded pursuit of excellence in some form is a substitute for forgiveness. It is counterfeit sanctification: an attempt at sanctification by the work of our own hands instead of the scarred hands of Christ. And it doesn't work. Broken, fallen creatures in a fractured world, we will eventually fail.

"But what about a perfect world?" we ask. "Surely Adam and Eve didn't get tired or forget in the Garden of Eden!" Perhaps not. But that doesn't make our limitations sin. Some of our failures may be brokenness that results from sin, but that does not make them sin. After the fall, thorns and thistles sprang up in the garden. The work became more difficult. But the thorns and thistles in our fields or in ourselves are not sin, but its aftermath. We may labor with brokenness in our lives. We may labor with limited energy, imperfect bodies, short memories, or low IQs. But that is not our sin, only our limitation. And God's promise for that is another face of grace. "My grace is sufficient for you, for my power is made perfect in weakness" (2 Cor. 12:9). God can work through our weakness, using our weakness and even our sins to accomplish his purpose of revealing himself in the world.

Looking back over this chapter, we see that we have two opportunities in regard to shame. We can sort guilt-shame from other shame and ask forgiveness. We also can uncover any false standards that cause nonguilt shame and seek freedom from that false standard and forgiveness for it. These are processes that last a lifetime, not instant accomplishments. They are an awakening, not an arrival. These are the processes which theology calls sanctification.

How can we separate guilt-shame from other shame? I have no magic formula, only a few tools to help you in the process.

1) Live close to the Word of God. Spend time with it.

Listen to it. Use it for light on your life's path and your life standards.

And use it for more than that.

In reading God's word, we cannot only look for divine shoulds, but we can recognize it as more than a shoulds list. In college when I was getting A's in course work and F's in self-esteem, I sought help from the campus pastor.

One of the things I confided, as the tears poured, was my lack of response to the Bible. "I read it and nothing happens. I don't know any more when I finish reading than when I start," I said. "I read a chapter and I think, 'So what?' "

Dr. Hulst took the Bible from his desk, opened it, and extended it toward me.

He said, "Remember, Carol, this is not just God's to-do list. It is also his love letter. Accept it as his love letter and read it that way."

Gradually, over the years, the love-letter concept has become part of the way I read God's record of his dealings with his people.

2) Spend time talking with the Lord. Tell him your goals and dreams, your failures and frustrations. Share your shame with him. Use the Serenity Prayer often: God grant me the grace to accept the things I cannot change, the power to change the things I can, and the wisdom to know the difference. Ask God to reveal his will in your life. And listen for his answer!

3) To combat societal pressure, be willing to risk a bit of eccentricity. You need not conform! You may find support in Christian friends who are also seeking to mold their standards to God's will, instead of the standards of our competitive, superficial, perfectionist culture.

4) Continually be creating an ideal or heroine who conforms to God's will for your life. Visualize an ideal capable of both work and worship, someone who accepts limits and doesn't feel threatened by mistakes. Visualize an ideal who balances her need for renewal with loving service to God and others. Visualize a heroine or hero asking God to lead her to

and through her task in life. Visualize a heroine who accepts forgiveness and who experiences it in her inner being.

For finding forgiveness and experiencing relief from guilt-shame, we can use some other tools. For excellence seekers, forgiveness is often a theological concept we hold in our heads, but don't experience in our lives. Some of the suggestions below may aid in that experiential relief.

1) Confess. You cannot be relieved of guilt-shame without confession. Confession doesn't mean excuses, and it doesn't mean presenting the super-you to God, telling him that super-you is the true you, and promising to do better tomorrow. Confession doesn't mean asking him to understand extenuating circumstances. It means, pure and simple, that you confess that you have violated his will and that you ask his forgiveness, based only on the work of Christ. Come just as you are, without one plea but Jesus' blood.

2) Read Romans 5–8 daily for several weeks. Read that section aloud. Read it silently. Read it slowly, read it fast. Let its message soak into your deepest soul. "Therefore, there is now no condemnation for those who are in Christ Jesus." No condemnation. No guilt. No reason for shame. Read those chapters in three different translations. Read them, substituting the personal pronoun "I" where Paul uses "we."

Read the words until you know in your heart that neither height nor depth, nor anything else in all creation (including your shortcomings, improprieties, and guilt), will be able to separate you from the love of God that is in Christ Jesus your Lord.

3) Learn to be silent. I don't mean just to stop talking. I mean to quiet the voices inside you and listen. I mean to hold your mind from its endless fluttering.

When you pay attention to the chattering internal voice and try to silence it, you will learn how hard silence is. The first time I tried this kind of meditation, it was hard on my faith. I read a book by Dorothea Brande, *Becoming a Writer,* in which she suggested quieting the mind before beginning writing. She suggested just focusing on one thing—a small object in front of you—and not letting any other thoughts intrude. Or just watch your thoughts skitter until they finally subside, she suggested. Seated at the library table, I tried it. My mind did skitter like a colt. But I focused, and slowly I could hold myself in stillness for a second, two seconds, then three. And that was the limit of my quietness span. But the sense of quiet and peace that came—and the subsequent concentration and energy—overwhelmed me. "This is the peace and power that comes from prayer," I thought.

It wasn't until later that I learned to couple that quietness with an experience of God's presence. Then I found new meaning in the verse, "Be still and know that I am God." I learned not just to silence my outer voice, but also the inner voices that clamored for attention. I learned that it is hard to listen for God's voice when all the inner voices are clamoring. I learned the gift of silence.

4) Harness the power of your imagination. When you read the great biblical stories of forgiveness, picture the events in your mind. Give the people faces, clothes, gestures, and environments.

At 20, I chose the books of Kings for my devotional reading. As I read I began getting powerful pictures of some of the scenes. When I read about Elijah departing this earth in a fiery chariot, leaving behind his mantle, I saw that red vehicle with flames—and for some reason skis like Santa's sleigh. When I read about the children taunting Elisha, "Go on up, you baldhead," I had a picture complete with robed children, a forest, and a small building. Those images leapt from the pages. With the images I could hear the rich, resonant voice of my childhood pastor. He had preached a series on Kings a decade earlier.

I had forgotten the theological conclusions he reached, but the pictures he had painted in his sermon series were still powerfully present with me. Such is the power of the imagination.

Harness that power! When you read the story of the prodigal son, picture the father running with open arms to welcome his wayward child. And then picture yourself as that child.

We are not just rational creatures. We are also imaginative ones, and we can harness that power for the experience of release from guilt.

5) Use the power of repetition. In *Space for God*, Don Postema suggested following the imaginative reading of the story of the prodigal son with repeating "I belong to God" for two minutes. Then he suggested slowly repeating that sentence for five minutes as part of daily devotions for a week.

"What a ridiculous idea," I thought when I first read his suggestion. But I respected his opinion, so I tried it. I said it over and over, loud and soft, slow and fast, excitedly and contentedly, with drama and with confidence. Sometimes when I did it I pictured myself as the returning prodigal held in my father's arms. And gradually the feeling came. Now when I repeat, "I belong to God," I am filled with a quiet sense of peace, because I know in my inner being that I belong to God.

The same can be done with another phrase. I like Don Postema's choice, because it captures the sense of belonging without focusing on sin and reinforcing shame. But if you preferred, you could repeat, "My sins are washed away through Christ."

The process of sorting guilt-based shame from other shame and of experiencing forgiveness is a continual process. The process may be especially strenuous for those of us who are excellence prone. But the biggest and first step is to realize that there is sorting to be done and that it is possible to be freed from guilt and shame. After that it is a process of gradual growth, of sanctification—not counterfeit but real. We learn that we don't need to be driven—we are forgiven!

9

Checking Your Roots

When baseball hitter George Brett, 10-time All-Star player with a seven-figure salary, finishes a game, what's on his mind? He says, "When I'm in the shower after a game or driving home from the ball park, I think about how my dad's going to be happy when he gets up and sees the paper the next morning. But if I do bad, he'll throw the paper or his coffee cup against the wall. It'll ruin his day."

George's father, who once kicked his young son for making two errors in a Babe Ruth League game, admits, "I was too tough on him, I really was. I'm sure after a while, he hated to go home."

And as an adult when George hit a three-run homer, what was his first response, tears streaming from his eyes? "Wouldn't it be great if Dad were here?"

George Brett has been formed by his childhood. We all have. Our childhoods affect our adult lives, sometimes more than we know. As William Wordsworth said, "The child is father of the man."

Sometimes the roots for our excellence standard lie deep in our past, further underground than we realize.

Psychologist Karen Horney said that children need

warmth, approval, and a certain amount of friction growing up. Without these, she stated, children develop a basic anxiety *(Neurosis and Human Growth)*. To compensate for this anxiety they form idealized selves, superselves, to which they constantly try to mold themselves in a sort of "search for glory." Their real selves are suppressed as inadequate, and the search for their ideal selves dominates their lives.

What sort of environments produce a search for glory, for an achieving superself?

Some excellence seekers simply grew up in homes where parents modeled high expectations of themselves. In *Living with a Perfectionist*, Dr. David Stoop wrote that some perfectionists have simply internalized parental values. Their parents were workaholics or perfectionists, and they followed the parental model. Their parents had high standards and they followed suit. "I grew up as the daughter of a small-town businessman," says Dorothy. "We had a strong sense of family and of what we did and didn't do. My parents simply assumed that we would dress well, have fine things, and have good manners."

Other excellence addicts, however, find that their standards are an attempt to please a demanding, never-satisfied parent. "If I got all A's and one B," says Jennifer, "My parents looked at the B and asked why I had gotten it." A criticism-oriented home such as this often fails to provide the needed sense of warmth, to satisfy a basic hunger for touch. This hunger is fed with the substitute food of achievement, and love becomes conditional. The message heard by a child is, "I will love you if you do well in school."

But even when they do well, they rarely hear the words "well done." They rarely see themselves as "good and faithful servants"—or good and faithful children. "I could never do domestic things well enough to please my mother," says Dorothy. "From the time I was eight until I turned eighteen, she always followed me around and added a little extra polish."

Sometimes the parents expected their children to fulfill

their own dashed hopes. "My mother had never gotten her nursing degree, although she always wished she had, so her dream was for me to be a doctor," said Sue. "She felt like a failure, and she wanted me to make up for that." For these parents their children become their life, and their identification is so close that they view their children's achievements as their own.

Parental demands for achievement are often stronger for the firstborn child. Studies of birth order show that firstborns are saddled with more expectations, demands, and restrictions from their parents than are middle-born or last-born children. In addition, the firstborn is often expected to be more responsible (after all, she is the oldest) and is placed in charge as baby-sitter when parents leave home. She is also held more responsible for resolving sibling squabbles. She is told, "Be reasonable, Jane. Your brother is only a toddler." Thus, firstborns tend to be more achievement-oriented, and more driven than children of other birth order.

Distant and demanding parents, however, are not the only ones who produce children who are excellence addicts. An unstable home environment may do so as well. Adult children of alcoholics, for example, often tend to be people driven to some form of excellence. Perhaps they thought they could avoid the worst of a drunken rage by being model children, by keeping the house in perfect order, by being super-responsible, by making their parents proud of how they did in school.

They lived in an uncertain world of mixed messages of love and hate. They were told to tell the truth, and saw their parents living a lie. They were told they were good kids, but were also told if it weren't for them their parents wouldn't be driven to drink.

With this uncertain environment, excellence sometimes looks like the answer. It can become a solution, not just for children of alcoholics, but for children in any home in which the parents are unstable or neurotic, in which the environment is unpredictable. An abusive or emotionally ill parent might also provide such an unpredictable environment.

In these environments children can choose several roles which use the excellence standard. Each kind of excellence seeker can arise from the same family, with different children taking different roles.

In his personal growth series *I Should Be Happy . . . Why Do I Hurt?* Earnie Larsen lists several roles which can be chosen in an alcoholic/neurotic family. Three roles excellence seekers choose are: perfectionism, workaholism, and caretaking. Perfectionists are people who are never happy with their accomplishments or satisfied with the appearances of things. Workaholics have a need to work nonstop and to construct their lives in such a way that their work is never done. Caretakers feel the need to be totally in charge of those around them.

Perfectionists live with unreasonable standards for the *quality* of their work. Workaholics have unreasonable shoulds for their work *quantity*. Caretakers tend to live by false responsibility shoulds. The perfectionist children desperately tried to relieve their anxiety through keeping their rooms and selves spotless. The workaholics tried to cook and keep the house for mom, and make the honor roll at the same time. The seven-year-old caretakers tucked a drunken father in bed and comforted a crying mother.

Although family structures are crucial in the formation of excellence seekers, other early experiences also may be formative. In Charles's childhood during the Depression days, he carried government issue milk from the firehouse to his home, accompanied by the jeers of his schoolmates. Out of that pain rose his drive toward economic security—an attractive car, stylish clothes, and the pastorate of a large, wealthy church.

Pecking order in the school classroom or a teacher's attitude toward grading may be formative. But for most of us, our early formation came primarily from our families, for the home was the hub of our existence.

Laura made an important discovery the day her counselor

asked her, "As you were growing up, who was responsible for whose emotional welfare—were you responsible for your mother's or was she responsible for yours?"

At first she was silent, rejecting the intuitive answer which immediately sprang to her mind. The silence lengthened. Finally she said slowly, "My instinctive response—a sort of gut level reaction—is that I was responsible for my mother's emotional well-being. But that's stupid. I wasn't. A child isn't responsible for a parent's emotional well-being. But that's how it felt—and how it feels."

In discovering those roots, she saw the source of her current feeling of total responsibility for the actions of her children. She was still living out her childhood caretaker role. When she identified the source of her role choice, she took an important step toward change.

As adults, we may still be living out the roles of our childhood and it may be helpful to go back and look at that childhood for the messages we absorbed as children. We are going to do that in a moment, but first we need to keep in mind several important principles for checking our roots.

1) You do not examine your roots in order to find a scapegoat for your current dead ends. You look at the past in order to understand your present behavior, and understanding, to have some tools for change. Earnie Larsen, in *I Should Be Happy . . . Why Do I Hurt?*, claims every person on earth has a life story that could be used as an excuse!

2) The absolute truth of your memory about your childhood is not crucial. What is important is how you heard and saw it. If your siblings heard and saw things differently, that is OK. What you heard and saw was what shaped you.

3) Share your understanding of the past with someone. The physical process of stating things aloud is helpful. And any feedback is a double bonus. Your listener need not be a professional counselor, unless you find your memories traumatic or frightening—as Marty did. When Marty began searching her past, she discovered she had repressed her memory of

being physically and sexually abused as a child. She had uncovered a monster for which she needed professional help.

How do you begin looking for the messages of your childhood? Perhaps a good way to start is just to relax and let your mind float back. Find half-a-dozen or so of your earliest memories. Jot them down. Having done that, you may want to follow a process similar to the one Earnie Larsen suggests in *I Should Be Happy . . . Why Do I Hurt?*

1) Ask yourself what was demanded of you in childhood. What were you expected to do? Also ask yourself what you were forbidden to do, what was not allowed. You may want to divide these questions into two columns—a column for actions demanded and forbidden by your mother, and for actions demanded and forbidden by your father. Jot down your answers. Give yourself time.

2) Jot down what message(s) you took away from these rules.

3) Jot down how these messages affect your current behavior and values.

This is not a five-minute exercise, but a process which may span several days or weeks in bits and pieces of time. If you have difficulty answering, it may help to simply spend more time recalling incidents and writing them down. Eventually you will see a pattern emerge from the incidents.

Here are some samples of the ways three people responded to these questions.

Neil: My parents didn't really have a lot of rules for me about behavior. I didn't have a curfew, for example. The only real rules I can think of were that we couldn't crunch carrots or sing at the table. The standards were much more underground than that.

What dominated my life was the fact that my father was very critical. Even before Sunday dinner, on the drive home, he was already criticizing the pastor's sermon. And it wasn't just the pastor, it was everyone. I can remember only two times in my life that he praised me.

I think as a result I worked very hard in order to protect myself from criticism. The message I got was: If you do something public, you can expect to be criticized—so cover all of your bases. I worked very hard to be above criticism. I had the longest activity list behind my name in the school yearbook. One year I could have been senior class president and student council president at the same time, but I turned one down because I thought people wouldn't like me if I did both.

So today, I work very hard to win people over. My standards change depending on who I am around. I adapt them to please others.

Dorothy: I grew up as the daughter of a small-town businessman. Everybody knew who the Andersons were, and we knew we had an identity and an image. We were always well dressed and carefully groomed. We took pride in having fine things and knowing good manners. We were the Andersons. Anything less than the best was not appropriate.

Without realizing it, the message I got was one of superiority, especially when I also started coming home with good grades.

Even today I have a hard time dealing with my own abilities. I don't know what to say when someone says, "Oh, you're so talented!" I still have high standards for appearance and clothing, although I cannot now afford to dress in the same way and have the fashionable, expensive clothing I would like. My first inclination is always: it has to be the best. I overprepare for any teaching or performing. The deadline arrives and I haven't yet finished preparing!

June: I was the oldest of four children and was expected to set a good example for the others. I was held up to them as a model student who should be imitated. We competed intensely.

My mother went through periods of depression when she

had a difficult time coping—and I listened to her crying and tried to be strong. My dad was easygoing, but he mostly wanted me to keep mom stable. In addition, my mother was very fearful of what people thought of us. A public flaw was forbidden.

The message I came away with was: achieve, be strong, win, and don't make mistakes.

That is still strong for me today. I have a strong need to be good at whatever I do and avoid tasks at which I won't excel. I am extremely competitive and see other people as threats. But I also have a strong need for their approval.

The backgrounds of each of these people differ, but all have a strong drive—a drive which sometimes makes them miserable. When Neil, who has published some half-a-dozen articles on electronics, isn't at work on one, he wakes in the middle of the night feeling worthless. When Dorothy hasn't finished preparing for a performance, and things don't go perfectly, she feels defeated. June rides a rollercoaster between needing to conform to people's expectations and competing with them.

However, Neil, Dorothy, and June have a choice now. As children they didn't. They chose the route of behavior which was needed for survival at the time. But if they see the roots of their values and how their current lives are blighted, they do have a choice. They are adults, not children. Without scapegoating their parents, they can examine the past in order to take action in the present. Learning new roles is possible.

A major step in breaking with your childhood is to separate your concept of God from your view of your parents. Your parents are not equal to God. Your parents were your first windows to God in representing authority. At two you saw them as gods. But now that you have become an adult, you can put away childish things. God can be separated from your parents.

God is not a demanding, distant, critical parent—he loved

you so much he sent his Son to die for you. God is not a needy, inconsistent authority who puts you in a double bind or sends mixed messages—God consistently loves, forgives, and guides if you are willing to be still and know that he is God. God does not expect you to erect a false front of a super-you, to appear worthy of his love—he loves the real you, just as you are. Just as you are through Christ, you are good enough—good enough to be loved, good enough to accomplish his purposes. All you have to do is be yourself, your real self. One day at a time you can work your way free by separating your concept of God from your childhood windows to him.

A second step is to realize your equality with your parents. You need to establish an equal relationship with them in actual life, and with them as you hear their expectations inside of yourself. The most important question is not, "What happened in childhood?" A more important question is, "What are you doing about it?"

You are no longer the child trying to earn parental approval through achievement. You are no longer the sibling supervisor if you choose not to be. You are not responsible for your parent's emotional welfare. You do not earn status for them by your achievements. They don't live through your accomplishments. And their criticism doesn't affect your worth. You no longer need to measure up to their standards and values, but to establish your own.

This doesn't mean you forget about your parents. You have a responsibility, as mentioned earlier, to make your peace with your parents or with your memory of them. Bitterness is a self-fueling fire that can burn within eternally until it consumes you. "Forgive one another just as God through Christ forgives you," the Bible tells us, and that includes parents. Forgiving doesn't mean being willing to play the old roles. It doesn't mean fulfilling your parents' dead dreams, providing for their emotional needs, living up to their models. But forgiving does mean being able to remember the past without anger. The ability to talk about an event without anger is one index to whether you have forgiven. To get there you may need to first recognize your anger, acknowledge it, and express it. Having done that, find ways to release it. Forgive as Christ has forgiven you.

The process of establishing equality forms new roots, but you find yourself still in the same family. A philodendron cutting does not become a coleus. But, philodendron or coleus, you need your own roots, your own direct pipeline to the living water, Jesus Christ—in whom you live and move and have your being.

By Christ's power, freedom from the tyranny of excellence comes. June says, "I finished playing a party game one Christmas and realized I had been playing the game for the sheer joy of it—not to win or to be best. What pleasure to be freed, for a moment at least, from the god of competition!"

Marty, who was sexually and physically abused, is still working on the process. She has anger to deal with and scars and pain. But she has discovered that she has a choice. And she has made her choice. She is healing. She cannot yet use the term *father* for God because of her abuse by her own father. But she has a love for the Lord, and she is healing. "It takes time," she says, "But I know that healing is possible. I am healing. Slowly, slowly, I heal."

Gradually, slowly, she grows her own roots, her own standards. Still a philodendron, shaped by her past, but no longer dependent on it.

With roots of our own, the past has been defused. It has lost its power over us. We can say to anger and bitterness as Jesus did to death—Where is your sting? Where is your victory?

With roots of our own we are freed from the search for glory Karen Horney wrote about. We are freed from the need for an ideal self. Instead, our real self is freed to *give* glory to God. We are freed to focus on our task of being his hands in his world, on our task of revealing his presence.

10

Enjoying the Moments

In Thornton Wilder's haunting play *Our Town*, a stage manager grants Emily's request to return from death to relive her 12th birthday. The day disappoints her. She begs her mother to look at her—really look at her—for just one moment.

Just before she returns to the cemetery, she asks the stage manager, "Do human beings ever realize life while they live it—every, every minute?"

He answers, "No. The saints and poets, maybe—they do some."

We excellence seekers would do well to listen to Emily's request to stop and really look. We usually are not among the saints and poets who realize life while they live it. We often forget that this moment is good enough to be experienced fully, to be savored, to be enjoyed.

Our quest for excellence is often not oriented toward the present but toward the future. We say to ourselves: When I get over this cold, I will. . . . When the kids start school, I will. . . . When the kids are out of the house. . . . When I get a job. . . . When I change jobs. . . . Tomorrow I will do better. Tomorrow I will be able to stay ahead of clutter. Tomorrow I will stick to my diet. Tomorrow I will be more patient.

We think we will start to live at some future date. As Paul Tournier says, we live our entire lives as if we are waiting for them to begin. Our drive to the mythical future prevents our savoring the present. It becomes simply a step to the future with no meaning of its own. It is simply a means to an end. I do the dishes so I can get to the laundry. I type the letter so I can get it in the mail. I read to my children to augment their verbal skills.

Each minute is a means to an end, meaningless in itself, simply a step to the future.

And that future never comes. It is a myth that remains in the mists of our imagination for the day when we arrive at our ideal selves. So we keep waiting for the dreamy moment when our problems dissolve and our flaws evaporate in one magic moment. That moment never comes. We have created a mythical future for our ideal selves.

Mythical futures sometimes require selective remembering. We have to erase part of our past in order to keep believing in our mythical future. My husband and I see an old friend about every half year. Whenever our paths cross, we summarize our past half year, telling each other where our lives have gone. Every six months we hear a new edition of the same story. It goes like this: "I have been so busy lately—too busy. I was put on the church building committee, and I'm in charge of Boy Scouts, and we're remodeling our house. I've had a really crucial project at work, too. But the projects are winding down in the next half year, and then I'll be able to relax a little more."

The next time we see him he tells the same story, but this time he's on the library committee, church council, and landscaping his yard. But he knows his life will definitely slow down after that. He's been telling us his overload is temporary for the past decade! He has a mythical future in which the load magically lightens without his saying no or making hard choices.

But said Sophie Kerr, "The future is now!" There is no mythical future. We shape our future by how we handle the present moment. When we realize that the future is now, we are able to make choices in this moment. In shaping this moment, we shape the real future for our real selves.

The future is now. Each moment, as it passes, has meaning. Each is unique and never repeated. Ecclesiastes tells us, "There is a time for everything, and a season for every activity under heaven: a time to be born and a time to die . . . a time to weep and a time to laugh . . . a time to embrace and a time to refrain."

Each moment has its place: the moment of beginning and the moment of closure, the moment of silence and the moment of shout, the moment of pain and of pleasure, the "I'm sorry" moment and the "I forgive" moment.

In each moment the real future for the real me is now. And, just as I am good enough, this moment is good enough. What does this mean? The fact that the future is now means you are not reading this book simply to get to the end, but you, at this moment, are seated in the presence of God. Knowing that the future is now, that each moment is the Lord's, frees us from seeing all of life as work.

A theatre professor at a college I attended demonstrated what it means to know the future is now. He arrived on campus before 7:00 each morning. When preparing a play for a performance, he was often on campus until 10:00 at night. He was hard-working and creative.

But religiously he refused to enter a single meeting or conference in the late afternoon. At 3:30 he left committee meetings or put down his marking pen and went home for a coffee break. Then he took his long-eared hound for a walk in the country. They ambled outdoors in any season. They crunched through fallen leaves and sogged through drizzle. He watched the creek freeze over, disappear under snow, and then reappear. He felt the wind on his face and the cold on his toes. He watched his hound gallop off in pursuit of a rabbit and disappear in the brush. He scratched the dog's ears when he returned, winded and woebegone.

He called his dog "Piphy." He had shortened the unlikely word *epiphany* and christened his lop-eared hound with it. As a college student I thought it was a preposterous choice of names. But looking back now, I approve.

An epiphany is a sudden grasp of the essential nature of something. It is also a manifestation of a divine being. Our knowledge of God, our sense of his presence often comes, not in those moments when we are grading papers or attending committee meetings, but when we stop work and "walk our dog"—whatever form that walk may take for us. We can experience epiphany. We can know in our bones that we have been remade good enough. We can know in our hearts how much God loves us, just as we are. We can be touched again by the eternal, and the future can be now.

To be touched by eternity in those epiphany moments is to know again the fifth dimension to our lives. We live, not just in the three dimensions of space and the fourth dimension of time, but also in a fifth dimension that extends toward our God. In those epiphany moments we discover again that the Lord is our shepherd. We discover again that we shall lack nothing. We discover again that we shall be—and are—good enough.

The fifth dimension gives meaning to the other four. It provides new motivation—but it is not just a refueling station for work. The epiphany moment does not exist to serve a mythical future!

Epiphany moments occur when we worship—in a pew, a woods, or an armchair. They can visit us while singing a hymn, reading God's Word, or praying. They can touch us when we touch our newborn's pinky or climb a tree. Our walks in the woods with Epiphany may be songs in the shower or devotional books.

The fifth dimension is always with us. But in this fractured and fallen world, we frail creatures need to set aside times to open our eyes to the fifth dimension: our Godward dimension. In *Space for God* Don Postema told how he used to write on his calendar 7:00–7:30 A.M.—prayer. Now he writes 7:00–7:30 A.M.—God. He added, "Somehow that's a little harder to neglect."

When I walk the trails through a woods, I rediscover life's fifth dimension. The trees were there long before I was born, and the rocks for even longer. And both will outlast me. I am an eyeblink in time, loved by their maker and mine. I am part of a whole. I am at peace. Epiphany lopes toward me barking with joy.

From worship, whatever form it takes, arises celebration. Revelation results in revelling. Playing follows praying as another form of touching eternity, of enjoying the moment, of letting life happen.

Doug taught me a lesson in letting life happen at a rehearsal warm-up for a college play. Before rehearsal the director arranged the play cast in a circle and picked up a huge, imaginary glob. He pretended to shape it into a top hat. He put the hat on his head and strutted around the circle. Then he handed it to a cast member on my right and said, "You change it into something else. Use it. Then pass it on."

I panicked. What would I make when my turn came? I looked around the room and saw a basketball hoop. I would make a basketball and shoot it. When my turn came, I did just that.

Others also quickly planned and then nervously shaped boxes, books, and gloves.

The blob was passed to Doug. Doug took it and played with it a few seconds. Some of the goo stuck between his fingers and he wiped them on his pants. He chewed a piece. It tasted putrid. He spit it out and kept on shaping. He played with that invisible blob and stretched and shaped and then surprised himself into creating a piano! He performed a stunningly complicated concerto on it and passed it on. And when he pushed it to his right, I could almost hear the castors squeak.

I had planned, and that's OK. But Doug had played and let himself go. He had given himself over to the moment. He hadn't known what he would make until he discovered it, in a moment of joy for him and for me.

In that moment Doug had experienced the gift of becoming as a little child. Jesus said that unless we become as little children, we cannot enter the kingdom of heaven. We usually say he meant we need to have childlike trust. But an outstanding quality of children is their ability to play!

Play and trust are closely related, however. To play is to trust the moment. To play is to trust that, even though this world is not perfect, the world has room for joy. To play is to trust the one who holds the future. It is to trust, with Corrie Ten Boom, the master weaver who sees the upper side of the weaving, while we see only the underside. We are free to play as children because we trust our Father, the master weaver.

In *When I Relax I Feel Guilty* Tim Hansel wrote this beautiful description of play: "Play is more than just nonwork. It is one of the pieces in the puzzle of our existence, a place for our excesses and exuberances. It is where life lives in a very special way. It is the time when we forget our problems for a while and remember who we are. Play is more than just a game. It is where you recognize again the supreme importance of life itself. . . . You can be whole again without trying."

To play is also to celebrate, to affirm, to say yes. To play is to say, "This is the moment the Lord has made. I will rejoice and be glad in it. I will take Epiphany for a walk beside a stream."

To play is to say to God, "It is good. It is enough."

In E. B. White's story "The Second Tree from the Corner," Trexler's psychiatrist asked him, "What do you want?" Trexler didn't know.

"What do *you* want?" he asked his therapist. The therapist wanted a wing on his house, more money, and more leisure.

That evening, walking along the street, Trexler answered the question for himself. "I want the second tree from the corner, just as it stands," he said.

White wrote, "And he felt a slow pride in realizing that what he wanted no one could bestow, and that what he had none could take away."

Since I read that story years ago, the second tree from the corner has become for me a symbol of affirmation, of yes. When I play, I am affirming, "I want the second tree from the corner, just as it stands."

In this fallen world we cannot say yes to everything. But neither is it totally ruined. God is in the process of redeeming it—and us. It is a glorious ruin. So are we. We are redeemed. We are good enough. We can say yes. We can celebrate. We can play.

We can chase soap bubbles with our toddler. We can imitate the owls calling to each other in our backyard at midnight. We can scrunch down in the brush in a game of hide and seek, unmoving as the seeker passes us six inches away. To play is to lose ourselves in a song instead of checking the program to see how soon the concert ends.

If you are an excellence seeker, you may find yourself with two nagging questions about play as revelling in the eternal. You may find yourself saying, "Yes, but what about work as part of life? Are you suggesting hedonism?" You may also find yourself saying, "I think we already live in a pleasure-mad society which doesn't need to hear this message at all."

Am I suggesting hedonism? Am I saying pleasure is all? Not at all. I'm just suggesting a little balance. We tell children, "Work before play," and that instruction is needed. Otherwise they would live only in the moment.

But we excellence seekers have turned that statement into an absolute standard—and the work is never done. We need to balance the work before play motto with one of equal value: save room for play!

We Christians with a strong work ethic have forgotten the religious dimension of play. We have forgotten that play touches eternity. We have forgotten the gift of good enough. We work unceasingly to earn it.

In answer to the second question, I don't think we really live in a pleasure-mad society at all. We do live in a society, however, which has assumed God's demise, a society with no eternity to experience, no moments of epiphany.

A society that acknowledges no fifth dimension is not really pleasure mad. It is simply externals mad. Want joy? Own a dream home. Want joy? Vacation in the Caribbean. Earn some joy—get a promotion. Or win some joy—win the softball game. Develop some joy—train your daughter to be a top gymnast.

Joy—a VCR. Joy—a thin body. Joy—a spotless room.

But joy is not external, it is internal. External joy sees only four dimensions. It doesn't understand a different way of being. It doesn't understand rejoicing in the second tree from the corner. It doesn't understand the gift of good enough.

A world without God cannot enjoy the moment of either revelation or revelling, the moment of praying or playing.

But we people good enough through Christ can!

If you find that joy is absent from your life, or only follows accomplishment, you may wish to try some of the options below for increasing your play and putting you in touch with the eternal.

1) Make a list of things you enjoy or think you would enjoy doing. Keep the pencil and paper handy. Throughout a day or so, jot things down as they occur to you. Jot down big things—a class in water color painting. Jot down smaller things—a walk around the block, a cup of pure grape juice, a novel you've been wanting to read, a phone call to an old friend.

Then read through the list and pick three you think you could do in the next week. Write them into your schedule and consider them commitments just as important as the rest of your plans.

Start out small. Don't make a major project or undertaking out of it. Simply take a few minutes for joy in a day.

2) Memorize the verse, "This is the day the Lord has made; let us rejoice and be glad in it." If you know the Scripture song using these words, sing them. If not, simply say them aloud.

I have found a revised version of that verse helpful. Whole days of joy are too big for me, so I usually sing, "This is the *moment* the Lord has made. . . ." (The Hebrew word for *day* refers simply to a period of time, not just a 24-hour period.)

Sing or say the words first thing in the morning. Say them when you feel an energy lag. Sing them when you find juice stains on the counter.

This is the moment the Lord has made. Sing it while caught in a traffic jam. Sing it while waiting after your son's allergy shots. Sing it when the telephone interrupts a good talk with your spouse. This is the moment . . . it will never return again. It is enough.

Sing it and celebrate a God who is not only Lord of the future, but also of the present. Celebrate the God of this moment and touch eternity.

3) Try scheduling a no-shoulds hour on Sunday afternoon. Write it in your agenda: no-shoulds hour. When the moment comes, follow where it leads.

A no-shoulds hour can be terrifying if you are comfortable only with a to-do list 18 inches long.

One Sunday when I scheduled it, I had to fight panic when the moment arrived. I had nothing on my agenda, and I wasn't allowed to consult my to-do list. Then my son asked me to play a board game. After that I decided to take a bike ride down to the nearby pond. A glass of juice on the deck filled the rest of the moments. I stumbled onto joy.

4) Memorize Tim Hansel's four commandments of contentment.

a. Thou shalt live in the here and now.

b. Thou shalt not hurry.

c. Thou shalt not take thyself too seriously.

d. Thou shalt be grateful.

5) Try playing a game to enjoy it instead of playing to win. Find games that are noncompetitive. Or play Scrabble or charades without keeping score. Simply revel in the words of Scrabble or the wordlessness of charades. Hit tennis balls to a partner without playing a game or keeping score. Just play for the joy of the game.

6) Shape a blob in any medium. Try taking a blob in your hands, visualizing it as dripping goo that shapes anyway you want and play with it. Let it become something in your hands. Don't *make* it become—*let* it become. That doesn't work for you? OK, get a box of crayons or markers. Close your eyes and scribble a design on paper. Then fill in the areas to make a pleasant pattern of color.

Try jotting down words as they occur to you. Just follow the trail of words and to where it leads you in a free-writing exercise. Or put on some music and move your body in the shape of the music. Let the movement happen instead of controlling it.

7) Read the following two selections daily for a week.

The first is from Josef Pieper's book, *Leisure, The Basis of Culture*.

Leisure is a form of silence, of that silence which is the prerequisite of the apprehension of reality: only the silent hear. . . . Leisure is not the attitude of mind of those who actively intervene, but of those who are open to everything; not of those who grab and grab hold, but of those who leave the reins loose and who are free and easy themselves—almost like someone falling asleep, for one can only fall asleep by 'letting oneself go.' When we really let our minds rest contemplatively on a rose in bud, on a child at play, on a divine mystery, we are rested and quickened as though by a dreamless sleep. . . . It is in these silent receptive moments that the soul of man is sometimes visited by an awareness of what holds the world together.

The second is a letter written by an anonymous friar late in life.

If I had my life to live over again I'd try to make more mistakes next time.
I would relax, I would limber up, I would be sillier than I have been this trip.
I know of very few things I would take seriously.
I would take more trips. I would be crazier.
I would climb more mountains, swim more rivers and watch more sunsets.
I would do more walking and looking.
I would eat more ice cream and less beans.
I would have more actual troubles, and fewer imaginary ones.
You see, I'm one of those people who lives life prophylactically and sensibly hour after hour, day after day. Oh, I've had my moments, and if I had to do it over again I'd have more of them.
In fact, I'd try to have nothing else, just moments, one after another, instead of living so many years ahead each day. I've been one of those people who never go anywhere without a thermometer, a hot-water bottle, a gargle, a raincoat, aspirin, and a parachute.
If I had to do it over again I would go places, do things, and travel lighter than I have.
If I had my life to live over I would start barefooted earlier in the spring and stay that way later in the fall.
I would play hookey more.
I wouldn't make such good grades, except by accident.
I would ride on more merry-go-rounds.
I'd pick more daisies.

I hesitated to make the seven suggestions above for fear you would see them as items for your to-do list, instead of recognizing them as entrances to another way of being. I hesitated to make a list of suggestions for fear you are like Rachel.

Rachel, who often feels pressured, told me a few days ago, "It's such a hassle. I have to get the kids' homework from the teachers before we leave. I have to line up substitute teachers for Sunday school, arrange for someone to watch the house and water the plants. I just don't know if it's worth all the trouble. I'm exhausted already. I'd like to forget it, but I suppose I should do it for the kids . . ."

What was she talking about? A winter vacation in the tropics!

Don't allow yourself to be pressured by the above suggestions. I'm not trying to add burdens to your life. They're just a ticket to a winter vacation in the tropics!

Praying and play, meditation and celebration, are one way to experience first hand the gift of good enough. They are not a barbaric yawp, but a quiet "yes" heard round the world. They are a way to realize life while we live it, not every moment, but at least some of them. Think again of the stage manager's answer to Emily's question, "Do human beings ever realize life while they live it?"

"The saints and poets, maybe—they do some."

Practice sainthood—stand in silent awe before your God. Practice sainthood—sing a song of praise in the shower. Practice sainthood—smell a lilac. Practice sainthood—jog through the snow. Practice sainthood—laugh with your toddler till your sides ache. Practice sainthood—revel in God's revelation all around.

Enjoy the moment. Enjoy the second tree from the corner just as it stands. It was placed there by your loving Father to whom you, and this whole world, belong.

11

The "I Am" Exercise and Other Tools

When God appeared to Moses in a burning bush and told him to return to Egypt to free his fellow Israelites from oppression, Moses questioned God.

> Moses said to God, "Suppose I go to the Israelites and say to them, 'The God of your fathers has sent me to you,' and they ask me, 'What is his name?' Then what shall I tell them?"
> God said to Moses, "I AM WIIO I AM. This is what you are to say to the Israelites: 'I AM has sent me to you.'"

What a strange answer! "I am has sent me to you." What a strange name! "I am who I am."

When I heard this story in Sunday school, I thought God must be teasing or joking. *Of course God is who he is,* I thought. *That's obvious. We all are who we are.*

Now, decades later, I begin to see some sense to God's reply. It's not obvious at all. It's an eternal mystery I will never fully understand.

God is who he is. The Hebrew verb used for *I am* carries with it a sense of timelessness. It means I was, I am, and I will be. God is self-existent. He is accountable to no one. He is totally other, always beyond my understanding, always the same.

The Hebrew verb for *I am* also carries with it the meaning, "to be an active, present reality," so that in other places in Scripture it is translated "came to," expressing God's felt and active presence. That presence is a second miraculous mystery: The great I am is present with us and within us!

When I search for my identity, I can never say, "I am," in the same sense God does. The foundation for my identity is always God. My "I am" is always framed by my being created and by my being redeemed.

I am not self-existent. I am not the great I am. I am made by God. And not only am I made, but—because I keep trying to deny my createdness, because I rebel, because I seek excellence in the pride of self-sufficiency—I also need to be redeemed. Christ died because of our drive for self-sufficient excellence.

My "I am" is not unchanging. My identity within that frame of being created and redeemed is always in process. Within that frame, I am not the same yesterday, today, and forever. I am not the same person I was at birth, at 10, or at 20. Neither am I the same as I will be 10 years from now. I am on a journey!

My "I am" is not all-knowing. I am not now the person I visualized 10 years ago. My vision for 10 years from now may not materialize.

As finite, changing creatures we keep asking who we are. The search is unending, because we are always in process. We are constantly redefining ourselves. When we take on a job on a community library board, we have redefined part of ourselves. When we become parents, or grandparents, our identity shifts.

Our search for identity is intensified by our rapidly changing society. We experience Alvin Toffler's future shock. We used to know who we were because of the unchanging institutions of which we were a part, but today we've lost that stable base for our sense of self.

Even in a world of future shock, though, the frame remains the same. We are created and redeemed. We are loved children of our Father, the great I Am.

With that foundation for our identity, we seek to know the details of who we are. And that knowledge eliminates any need for false modesty or pride in our search for self. Whatever we have is a gift twice over. That given-ness leaves no reason to deny what we have, or to believe that we have reason to be proud. God is the great I Am. Our "I am" is all gift.

What we need to do is simply be ourselves—our created and redeemed selves. One pastor I know uses this as a consistent counseling tool for discouraged Christians who feel inadequate: "Just be yourself," he says. "What you are in Christ is good enough."

When we lack a sense of "good enough," it is often because we have an ideal self to whom we have not measured up. We've seen in previous chapters that the ideal self is a tyrant filled with shoulds. We've also seen how the ideal self can keep us living for the mythical future. The time has come to take a closer look at this ideal self.

The ideal self dwarfs our sense of good enough. Our ideal self never tires, never makes mistakes, is always loving and giving, has multiple talents and infinite knowledge.

Our ideal self is sometimes a strange and contradictory mixture. Our ideal self may spend 24-hour days as supermom and also spend 24-hour days pursuing an exciting career. Our ideal self can handle a 48-hour day. Our real self can't. Our ideal self always wins any competition, but also consistently puts others first.

Our ideal self often does not conform to Scriptural guidelines. I find it fascinating that Jesus was God's sinless, ideal, perfect Son—and his contemporaries didn't recognize it. His parents scolded him for staying in the Temple. His followers disapproved of his dinner with Zacchaeus. The Pharisees found him so offensive they plotted his death. And his disciples, looking for a political ruler, thought his death signaled failure. When God's sinless Son walked this earth, he wasn't even recognized. His contemporaries had a different ideal!

Our ideals, too, may prevent us from recognizing Jesus. Our pride-filled, sin-smeared ideals may block our view of him and hamper our loving service.

Even our loving service, however, can become the tyrant of an ideal self! In *Love Within Limits* Lewis Smedes comments, "If we feel we must love with the energy of an angel, the vision of a prophet, the intellectual power of a genius, and the virtue of a saint, we will be frustrated lovers."

The ideal of living totally for God and for others is one many Christians struggle with. How can they balance self-denial and self-realization? They find themselves feeling guilty doing things for themselves because of their loving service ideal.

Perhaps the dilemma can be resolved by an illustration. A very generous and giving woman wrote out many checks to charity. And when the account was empty, she kept writing out checks to charity. But the checks were no longer any good. In order to keep giving, she had to keep money in the account.

In order to keep serving and loving, we need to keep replenishing our physical, social, and emotional checking accounts! Then we can keep on serving. Then we can keep writing checks.

God's instructions are, after all, to love our neighbor *as ourselves*.

Some of us, however, are in little danger of overdrawing our account. We're trying to accumulate millions. It may be millions of dollars, a million admirers, or millions of servants. We're headed single-mindedly for self-realization. Whatever our ideal self, Lewis Smedes reminds us, "We cannot love well if we are forever locked into a losing argument with the imperfect reality of what we are."

Our search for identity, then, has two parts: first, to find the real self sometimes obscured in our search for the ideal, and second, to accept that real self and serve God as we are. When we have found and accepted our real selves, we can treat our ideal selves with a sense of humor. When we have found and accepted our real selves, we can step off the emotional roller coaster which peaks when we deceive ourselves into thinking we can achieve our ideal, and plummets when we realize we can't.

How do you find your real self—your created-and-redeemed-by-God self? If you've been constantly aiming for an ideal self, you may not have a clear sense of self. If you've been living your life regretting the youthful dream you didn't live up to, you may not know who you are at this stage of your life.

The I am exercise is a step in the direction of finding and accepting your real self. The I am exercise takes time. It also is most effective if you actually perform the suggested activities instead of just reading about them. Reading them, you may have a rational understanding, but not an experiential one. Reading the I am exercise will not be the same as doing it.

Perhaps you'd like to proceed this way. Read to the end of the exercise and then make a decision. Do you think you would benefit from the exercise? Go for it! Does your real self want to invest the time? Do it! You don't feel you would benefit? That's fine, too. Don't berate yourself for not pursuing every option. You can serve God with your real self without doing this exercise. Before God's face, make the choice you see best for your real self.

If you choose to do it, you will need four sheets of paper, a pencil, a couple of bright, felt-tipped markers, a match, and 70 minutes.

Step 1: Preparation (10 minutes)

To see your current life in context, create a framework for the present.

On the first sheet of paper (Sheet 1) write the earliest memory you can think of at this moment. Then write one other memory from your life before you were 12. The first that pops into your head is as good as any. Write a vivid memory from your life between 12 and 20. (Don't agonize to find the most vivid, just write the one that surfaces.)

Now stop and think a moment. What was the most significant event in your life before 12? Between 12 and 20? Write both of them in a sentence or so.

One final question: At 20, how did you picture yourself at your current stage in life?

You've just created a mini-portrait of the past that formed you. You've completed the warm-up.

Step 2: *Who are you? (10 minutes)*

At the top of the second page (Sheet 2) use your marker to print, in half-inch letters: I am God's (daughter or son), created and redeemed. I am:

At the top of the third page (Sheet 3), print in half-inch letters: I am God's (daughter or son), created and redeemed. I am not:

Now read the two quotations below.

"To give up one's pretensions is as blessed a relief as to get them gratified."

William James

"It's great to be great, but it's greater to be human."

Will Rogers

On Sheet 2 complete the I am sentence over and over. Say to yourself "I am—" and write what comes to mind. Use adjectives (tall, shy), nouns (a chess player, a good listener), or verbs (able to swim).

If at any time you find yourself thinking of someone you should be, or of something you are not, list those shoulds or shortcomings on Sheet 3. Then go back to Sheet 2 and keep going. When the "I am" sentences stop coming, look at the questions below and keep going. Each time your mind runs dry, consult another question. (Write small. You may run out of space.)

• Who are you physically? (You may want to include details about your age, appearance, health.)

• Who are you in your relationships? (You may want to make statements about your relationships to family, friends, church members, community, country.)

• Who are you emotionally? What sort of temperament do you have?

• Who are you financially?

• Who are you in your occupations or working roles? What services or products do you provide?

• What other talents or gifts do you have?

• Who are you morally?

Keep going until you run out of material.

Step 3: Who are you not? (10 minutes)

You may have some sentences on Sheet 3 already from shoulds which surfaced in the previous step. Simply continue. Say "I am not—" and write what comes to mind.

This list could, of course, be infinite. There are hundreds of skills, relationships, occupations which are not yours. The focus of this list includes: 1) What you are not that you feel you should be, 2) qualities you choose to avoid, and 3) past dreams you haven't fulfilled.

With that in mind, begin. When your mind runs dry, use the questions from the "Who are you?" list, but simply change them to "Who are you not?"

At this stage you may be feeling a bit blue. The list of negative things you are and positive things you are not may seem overwhelming. Hang on! Help is on the way.

On the other hand, you may be feeling a warm glow of pride. You've just described a talented and upright person.

You're far above average—better than many people you know. Hang on! Help is on the way for you, too.

Step 4: Separating the sins (10 minutes)

Go through the two lists and copy onto Sheet 4 any items from those lists which you consider to be sins against God. Ask yourself which items on the list are disobedience to his guidelines for life. (Remember: It is no sin to be finite or have limits.) If you copy an item onto Sheet 4, draw a line through it after you have copied it.

Step 5: NAP time (10 minutes)

Take Sheet 2 again. And do the NAP exercise with it. In the left margin identify each statement with an N, A, or P, depending on how you feel about that statement.

N = Neutral
A = Ashamed
P = Proud

Now read aloud each statement marked P, and immediately after say aloud, "It is a gift of God."

Read each item marked A aloud, and immediately after say, "In Christ I am good enough for any task he calls me to."

Repeat this entire step for Sheet 3.

Step 6: Becoming whole (10 minutes plus a lifetime)

Use a wide-tipped marker (red if you have it) to write across the "I am" and "I am not" sheets in imperfect, inch-high letters diagonally: "I am created and redeemed by God. I am good enough, no more, no less."

Step 7: Expiation (10 minutes plus a lifetime)

Read each statement from your page of sins (Sheet 4) aloud. After each pray, "Father, forgive me for Christ's sake."

Then crumple the sheet in your kitchen sink and, if possible, light it with a match and watch it go up in smoke. Otherwise, shred the sheet and flush the pieces down the toilet. Your sins have disappeared forever. If you burned the sheet, you may wish to gather the ashes, carry them outside, and let the wind scatter them. Recite to yourself, "As far as the east is from the west, so far has he removed my transgressions from me."

File Sheets 2 and 3 in a convenient location, and go about your work and worship. When your eight-year-old beats you at the memory game, when you don't get the job you interviewed for last week, take out the sheets and refresh your memory. Or if you get a job that 100 people applied for, you might also want to read them.

Why go through this process instead of just reading about it? Because 1) it forces you to clarify your thinking, and 2) it makes grace experiential. Theology about forgiveness and grace needs to become internalized, and the I am exercise is one way to do that.

Here ends the I am exercise. Make your decision about using it. If you opt to do it, get out the paper and equipment and begin. If you opt not to, read on.

Other options for finding and accepting your real self are also available:

1) Make a list of tasks done well and tasks done poorly in a day. Make them equally long. On a day you are feeling proud and at the peak of the roller coaster, you will have a hard time with the "done poorly" list. On a downhill day you will have trouble with the "done well" list. Balancing the list will smooth the roller coaster and lend stability to your life.

2) If you don't like making lists at day's end, live by the equal time rule. Every time you knock yourself for a failing— aloud or silently—take time also to compliment yourself for a strength.

3) Practice accepting compliments graciously. Check your emotional temperature after a compliment. Are you feeling proud? Turn things around. Tell your complimenter, "Thank you," and tell them it's nice of them to say that. Are you tempted to deny the compliment and put yourself down? Stifle the words. Simply say: "Thank you. It's nice to hear that." You may also want to check your compliment filter. Do you

find yourself doubting the sincerity of the speaker? That's a roundabout way of letting your ideal self get the upper hand.

4) If you find yourself feeling blue, living in the shadow of your scolding, ideal self, take inventory at the end of the day. Sit down and take time to review what you did for the day. Don't just think, "I accomplished nothing today." Make a list of what you did. And everything counts. That relaxation with your feet up? It counts. That breakfast you made, those calls you made at the office, the book you read to your youngster, the repair work you helped a neighbor with—count them all. You may find that you did more than you feel you did. You may feel a little less of a failure for the things that didn't get done.

5) Is the perfectionist, ideal self still holding tyranny over you? Make an antiperfectionism sheet as therapist Dr. David Burns suggested in *Feeling Good: The New Mood Therapy.* List the jobs you plan to do and predict your enjoyment of them in a percentage scale of 1–100. When you finish the jobs, rate your actual enjoyment on the same scale. Finally, rate the percent of perfection you achieved on each job. The results may surprise you. When a perfectionist physician completed the sheet he found 99% enjoyment fixing a broken pipe which he did with only 20% effectiveness! Pleasure is not always in proportion to perfection.

6) If you berate yourself for failing to live up to your ideal self, try treating yourself as well as you treat others. Do you give yourself permission to criticize your friends frequently and without mercy? Perhaps not. You don't have permission to do that to yourself either. William Diehm claims that self-criticism should be as rare as self-surgery! He may be using hyperbole, but you do have the right to treat yourself with the same respect you treat others.

7) Harness your imagination short term instead of long term—for your real self in the present instead of for your ideal self in the mythical future.

If you check yourself, you may find that you set up vivid

daydreams in which you do everything wonderfully with your ideal self. That imagination is a powerful tool. Harness it; let it help you.

You have guests coming for a party this evening? When you wake, take a few extra minutes in bed and picture yourself readying the house and food well in advance of the deadline for their arrival. Picture yourself enjoying the preparation, not feeling pressured. Then picture yourself going to the door to welcome them—and really feeling glad to see them. Picture your day with details. See the rooms. See yourself working. What are you wearing? How are you feeling? Picture yourself calm, relaxed. What are you saying to your spouse and children?

Then review the images occasionally through the day.

The key, remember, is to harness your imagination in service of your real self, short term. This isn't daydreaming. It's creative planning!

8) Continue some form of journal writing on a regular basis. We've looked at several forms in previous chapters: challenging the shoulds, finding your roots, and now the I am exercise.

Your journal can continue some of these forms, or it can include others. You can simply write a trail of words as it comes to you. You can write prayers, problems, feelings, praise, records of events or conversations. You can write never-to-be-sent letters. You can write in any form that creates a record of your outer and inner life.

Marty has kept a journal for the 20 years of her marriage, through serious illnesses and loss of jobs. She says sometimes she reads through the record of previous years and then says to her husband, "Remember this? We lived through this and we survived. I think we'll survive the present, too."

A journal can provide that kind of comparison and encouragement from survival of the bad times. It can also provide inspiration from your moments of epiphany (your "aha" moments). They can be your own ministry to yourself when you are in the pit of despair.

However, if the discipline of journal keeping is not for you, you are in good company. C. S. Lewis said he found that a diary never included the significant things in his life. He gave it up because, looking back, he realized that he didn't know which events in his life were significant until later.

The preceding I am exercise and the eight subsequent suggestions are tools to find peace with your real self. Following your revolt against the tyranny of the ideal self, you may begin to see that there is more to life than self-realization. You begin to see beyond identity. You begin to ask questions about your niche among the worker-worshipers. You begin to ask questions about your form of loving service.

For there's a step that comes after the I am exercise, and that's the step of finding your tasks and losing yourself in them. Whoever loses his life for Jesus' sake shall find it, the Bible tells us.

From time to time it becomes necessary, though, to return to the question of identity in order to continue in service. When you reach another stage of life or have a setback, you may need to rediscover who you are. And that search for identity has always the goal of loving service, not just to discover self for the sake of self, but self for the sake of service. I seek to discover who I am in relation to the great I Am.

12

A Body, Not a Ladder

Winning isn't everything," said Green Bay Packers coach Vince Lombardi. "It's the only thing."

In our competitive culture, winning is important to us all. When we call ourselves the human race, we take that term literally.

Our need to win is most obvious, perhaps, in sports. A recent national college basketball championship game was a classic. The teams were so well-matched that often only a single point separated them. In the closing second a final basket determined the tournament winner—by one point. After the game the elated winners leaped, hurrahed, and hugged each other on the gymnasium floor, surrounded by fellow students and well-wishers. They hoisted the winning point maker on their shoulders and ran triumphantly toward the dressing room.

Then the TV cameras zoomed in for a closeup of a couple of losing team members. They drooped on the bleachers, backs slumped, elbows supported on their thighs, looking at the floor and mopping their faces with towels. Every movement was slow, dejected, despairing.

They had placed second in the nation by one point and they were in despair. Second place simply wasn't good enough for them. Second place felt like failure.

But competition is not limited to basketball tournaments. Competitive people treat life like a tournament in which their sole object is to get to the top.

We treat life like a tennis ladder. In a tennis ladder, I can challenge one of the players immediately above me to a match. If I win, I can place my name above hers. I can continue to challenge the players above me and continue to move up as long as I keep winning. If a challenger from below wins a match with me, her name goes above mine.

Marilyn often turns life into a ladder. She admits, "When I walk into a room, I can predict how comfortable I am going to be there in the first five seconds, based on where I fall in the ranks. And the question I ask myself in that first five seconds is, 'How can I get to the top of the heap?' I ask that question about whatever criterion is present at the moment. It can be athletics, intelligence, clothes, appearance. It doesn't matter. My first question is: How can I get to the top of the heap?

"If I go to the pool to swim laps and most of the women there are senior citizens who will rest after each lap while I keep going, I'm comfortable. If I walk in and see athletes who will swim three laps to my one, I'm uncomfortable."

Sometimes we make those comparisons even when there is no interaction, when we are simply people-watching at a restaurant or airport, or pushing our shopping cart down the grocery store aisle. June says her internal monolog at a grocery store is sometimes a string of evaluations and rankings that accompany her through the store aisles. Her monolog goes like this: Why does she use all those silly coupons? Doesn't she know she's perpetuating a wasteful system? . . . My, but she's overweight. She really could lose a few pounds. . . . And that woman really should do something about her hair before she shows up in public. . . . Can't she keep her kids under better

control? I hate to see someone angry with children in public.
. . . She looks sophisticated. She just came from her office to
pick up a few things, I guess." When June gets to the so-
phisticate, she suddenly becomes aware of the peanut butter
spot on her coat and of her overdue haircut. June is competing
for ladder position as she pushes her cart through the grocery
store.

June takes her ladder with her when she goes home as
well. She even uses a ladder rung for the bottom of her fry
pan.

She says, "When my mother-in-law visits, she inevitably
tries to clean the baked-on grease from the bottom of my frypan—with little success. And when we wash the saucepan that
used to belong to my husband's grandmother, she tells again
with pride the story of how shiny Grandma always kept that
pan.

"It doesn't shine in my house, and she never succeeds in
getting the brown stains from the bottom of my electric fry
pan, no matter how hard she tries."

June reacts in one of two ways to the dilemma of the
frypan, although she says neither of them to her mother-in-
law. She either reacts in superiority, as if she's higher on the
ladder, and thinks, "What a useless way to be investing time.
I have more important things to do with my minutes and hours
than invest them in shining the bottoms of my pans."

Or she reacts as lower on the ladder, thinking, "I know.
I really should do a better job of keeping my pans shiny. They
really don't look as nice as they could. My housekeeping just
isn't up to par."

This past Sunday I used a ladder at Sunday worship. Our
guest pastor was a missionary whose standards for language
did not meet mine. I winced when he began a sentence or two
with, "I seen. . . ." He preached about when Paul and Silas
were in prison and the doors miraculously opened. Paul and
Silas didn't use their opportunity to escape, but sat in their

cell and sang. He commented, "I like to think that one of the songs they sang was 'Amazing Grace.' "

"Amazing Grace?" I thought. *"Amazing Grace?"* Where is his sense of history? Doesn't he realize 'Amazing Grace' was written by John Newton about 18 centuries *after* Paul and Silas? Where is his sense of history?"

I sat in smug superiority, a step higher on the ladder.

That afternoon I read a book by a popular Christian writer who referred in passing to having read all the volumes of *Gulag Archipelago,* a large book of Celtic Prayers, and a four-book series, *The Raj Quartet.* I hadn't waded through more than a short excerpt of *Gulag,* and I hadn't even heard of the other two works.

I had heard her speak at a conference several months earlier, and her list of recommended reading had left me paralyzed. I felt inferior, defeated. In the anger of that defeat I tried to reestablish superiority. "Where does she get all this extra time to read all of that?" I wondered. "Does she really remember any of it when she's done?" Then I felt defensive. "Oh, well, I don't really think I want to read *Gulag Archipelago* and *The Raj Quartet* anyway. Who needs them? They're just for esoteric, intellectual snobs, and I don't want to be one of those."

But I still felt defeated. I was lower on the intellectual ladder.

For excellence seekers, competition can be a way of life. We may change turf, but coming out on top is what matters. When we were students, it was being at the top of the class. Now that we have graduated, it has become making the most money, being the best mother of toddlers, being the trimmest 40-year-old, the most successful at reentering the job market. Which game doesn't matter. We change that to suit our life stage. It is the coming out on top that matters.

If our standard is the ladder, we may see ourselves in one of two ways: as winners or as losers. When we see life as a vertical scale and ourselves as losers in the competition, our self-esteem suffers. Our sense of worth vanishes. Some people who claim they are not competitive simply see themselves as losers in the competition and give up. They just curl up in their corners and say, "I can't compete. I'm not good at things, and therefore I won't try. Don't ask me to do it." They have given up, but they still have a ladder concept of life. They simply see their position as bottom-rung losers. They may feel like praying Erma Bombeck's prayer, "Lord, if you can't make me look thin, then make my friends look fat."

When we see ourselves as winners, we tend to overestimate the height of our rung. Studies show, for example, that high school students asked to rate themselves in such qualities as athletic ability or intelligence rarely rated themselves below average. But that sort of bias is not limited just to students. A survey revealed that 94% of the surveyed group of professors considered their teaching to be above average.

The same sort of overestimation occurs in marriage. In one survey married people gave themselves more credit for child care and household chores than their spouses gave them. David Meyers used the example of his family clothes hamper. Every night, he said, he and his wife pitch their clothes at the bedroom hamper. In the morning one of them picks up the clothes and puts them inside. They discovered, to their surprise, that both of them thought they picked up the clothes 75% of the time! ("The Inflated Self," *The Christian Century*, Dec. 1, 1982.)

Most of us ladder climbers, however, don't see ourselves as complete winners or losers. We alternate in our estimation of our standing. And, like Marilyn, our comfort level depends on our estimation of our standing in that first five seconds upon entering a room.

We realize, too, that cutthroat competition is not socially acceptable, and we find ways to disguise our climb. The title of the best-seller was not *In Search of Superiority*, which would be blatantly competitive. It was *In Search of Excellence*. Because excellence carries so many meanings, we can disguise our ladder climbing under another name if we wish. We can call it excellence when we really mean superiority.

Women, especially, are covert about competing. Our culture has been competitive, but we idealized a noncompetitive image for women. Women didn't stop competing, though; we simply sent the competition underground. We do compete. We subtly compare ourselves to each other in matters of appearance and child rearing, in matters of intelligence and articulateness, in grooming and weight. And some of us, throwing off past cultural moorings, have become more openly competitive.

The ladder image for life, the competition model, for both men and women, is, however, one very real face of the drive for excellence. It is part of the same package. We pile comparison "shoulds" on ourselves. We live in the mythical future when our ideal self will always be the winner in any sort of competition. We fail to accept who we are unless we win. Our excellence standard calls for victory over the competition.

C. S. Lewis saw a close link between our competitive spirit and our pride. He claimed, in fact, that pride is essentially competitive. In *Mere Christianity* he wrote, "Pride gets no pleasure out of having something, only out of having more of it than the next man. . . . Once the element of competition has gone, pride has gone. . . . If I am a proud man, then, as long as there is one man in the whole world more powerful, or richer, or cleverer than I, he is my rival and my enemy."

The solution to pride, as it appears in our ladder concept of life, is not to climb higher. The solution is not to get to the top. Neither is the solution to gracefully accept our rank on one of the low rungs. The solution to the dangers of the ladder is to throw away the ladder altogether.

Because of God's gift of good enough, we are not climbing a ladder. We good-enough people are part of a body—the body of Christ. Paul told the Corinthian Christians the importance of that body. "For we were all baptized by one Spirit into one body . . . Now the body is not made up of one part but of many. If the foot should say, 'Because I am not a hand, I do not belong to the body,' it would not for that reason cease to be part of the body" (1 Cor. 12:13,14).

Good-enough people are not climbing a ladder, but they are part of a body. Did you hear what Paul said? "God has arranged the parts in the body, *every one of them,* just as he wanted them to be." The hand and eye and foot are all necessary parts of the body. He has given the gift of seeing to the eye and the gift of grasping to the hand.

The body concept eliminates the need for both pride and for low self-esteem. We are free to see both our neighbors' talents and our own as different skills, all needed in the body.

The attitude of the body parts is this, says Paul, "That its parts should have equal concern for each other." Closely linked with the body concept is the ideal of servanthood. The parts of the body exist, not to compete, but to serve. Servanthood was the object lesson Jesus taught when he washed his disciples' feet. His death was the ultimate servanthood.

So, too, we body parts are servants to the body. We don't repeat Christ's sacrifice and we don't all wash feet, but each of us uses our gifts to serve the body and its head, Jesus Christ. Our responsibility as good-enough people is to replace the image of the ladder with a body, the body of Christ.

The body gives June a new option in her dilemma about pan bottoms. She has another option besides telling herself that clean pan bottoms are female slavery, or that she should be a better pan keeper. She can drop the vertical scale. For June's mother-in-law, shiny pans are a source of joy. For her, shining pans provide an aesthetic satisfaction in the polished surfaces. But for June that is not the case. She sees the pans as strictly functional. If the pans are clean enough to be sanitary, that's good enough for her.

June can accept the fact that she and her mother-in-law are using different standards and the pans fulfill different purposes for the two of them. She can exchange the image of a ladder for the image of members of a body.

I can do the same with sermons which are missing a few auxiliary verbs and place hymns in the wrong century. The missionary who made the errors had worked for 23 years among America's poor, jobless, and alcoholics. If he had been the kind of person given to perfection in language or fine points of history, he might not have had an effective ministry among them. But instead, he had been an effective and caring part of the body of Christ.

The speaker who reveled in obscure books is also part of Christ's body with me. Perhaps it is her task to read those obscure books in order to find relevant material for today's women in today's world. The world needs culture keepers to delve into books of Celtic prayers. She was just working as part of the body.

But what about the basketball tournaments and tennis ladders? How do we substitute a body for those? It's less obvious, but even my tennis ladder is not really a ladder—unless I allow it to be. And my opponent is not truly my opponent but my ally. How could a tennis player develop the skills of the game, enjoy the thrill of a well-placed lob or volley, if she had no opponent? The thrill of tennis demands an opponent, as an ally for playing the game.

The tennis ladder aids us in finding the opponents best qualified to help us. For we play our best and most enjoyable games when we play an opponent who is closely matched to our skill level—in any sport. So the ladder is a system for helping us to find that level in order to assist our enjoyment and skill level in the game. Even a tennis ladder can be a servant to the body, not a tool for identifying winners and losers.

But life has deeper losses than sports competitions. We compete for jobs and promotions. What do we do when we interview for a position we really want and the job is offered to someone else? What do you say when your friend's daughter is accepted into medical school and your daughter is not? Aren't there real positions on a real ladder?

Facing such losses brings grief and requires time to find new directions for our lives. Deep wounds take time to heal.

Even deep wounds, however, don't require a ladder concept of life. The person offered the position is not higher on a ladder, simply more suited for work as that part of the body. The position does not give more worth or place them higher. It is simply a different body function, a function you are not called to at this point in history. We are a different part of Christ's body, serving in a different way.

The Bible does use other images to describe life, images which may seem competitive: a race and a fight. Although the Bible uses the images of a race for the Christian life seven times, the emphasis of those references doesn't lie in their competitive element. Their emphasis lies in the self-discipline and pressing on toward the goal of the high calling of God. In Acts 20:24 Paul writes, "I consider my life worth nothing to me, if only I may finish the race and complete the task the Lord Jesus has given me—the task of testifying to the gospel of God's grace." The race is to testify to grace, to tell the story of good enough!

When the Bible talks about life as a fight, it uses the term in two ways: for the good fight of faith and for the fight against evil. Paul advises Timothy to fight the good fight of the faith, after describing it as pursuing "righteousness, godliness, faith, love, endurance and gentleness." That's hardly a competitive model for life.

There is a competition all right, an all-too-real fight, but not with our fellow created-and-redeemed humans. It is a fight with evil, chaos, and hatred. It is the battle for holiness, righteousness, love.

The real fight is not to climb the ladder of worth. The real effort is to live as the parts of the body of Christ who have received the gift of good enough, and, as members of that body, to reach out and tell others of that gift. Our race is to tell the good news that life is not a ladder but a body. The fight is against the ladder itself!

What are some practical steps to take in eliminating our

ladder style of life? What can we do to experience our membership in the body?

Awareness of our gift of good enough is crucial to taking down our ladders. And we have looked at ways to do that in previous chapters.

Being aware of the gift of good enough, you can begin identifying your ladders. Are you using a ladder when you walk into your friends' brand-new, exquisitely decorated home—and either judge their materialism or feel twinges of jealousy? Are you using a ladder when your acquaintance home-schools her children and you feel guilty about the relief you experience when yours board the bus at 8:00, or do you disapprove of her failure to meet their need for socialization? Are you using a ladder when an acquaintance gets a promotion—and you either judge that he didn't deserve it or feel guilty because you didn't get one? Identify your ladders.

Having identified a ladder, eliminate it. You may wish to imagine yourself on a ladder rung and your acquaintance on a higher or lower one. Then take a huge eraser and wipe out that picture. Replace it with members of a body. Place your friend as one part of the body and yourself as another.

Continue to remind yourself of the importance of the body concept by reading 1 Corinthians 12:12-31 often. Notice how it precedes Paul's marvelous outpouring on the supremacy of love in Chapter 13.

If the phrase "I belong to God" has become a meaningful repeated image for you, you may find it also useful in group settings. Seated in church, or at a Bible study group, or a family picnic, remind yourself, "I belong to God in this setting, too." You may even shift pronouns and repeat to yourself, "We belong to God." When that knowledge penetrates your heart, the ladder leaves.

Finally, you may want to create a Perfectionists Anonymous group. You can cooperate with your group in body living and in erasing ladders.

You could begin by simply posting a note on your church

bulletin board: "Calling All Perfectionists. Calling All Perfectionists." I suspect you'd get a response. At a recent conference when I posted a notice asking for volunteer perfectionists to help with my research, I received half-a-dozen carefully printed or typed replies from volunteers eager to share their lives. You may find the same.

If you prefer to be less public about it, you can look over the congregation before church and find the people uncomfortable in a crowd. Look for the people who are worrying because they forgot to check the back of their hairdo before leaving home. Or find the women who always check their appearance in the church powder room before entering the sanctuary. Or find the members who are quiet in groups because they wait to say just the right thing. Or the people who serve on a dozen committees because they can't say no.

Tell them you're thinking of forming a self-help group for do-it-all people who want to develop as good-enough people. Then, after you've found four to six such people, you can hold your first meeting. You can introduce yourselves: "I'm _____, and I'm a do-it-all-aholic." Then you can cooperate as members of the body in helping each other find freedom from overcommitment. You may wish to work through this book together, or you may wish to choose a different format.

Sharing your walk with fellow Christians, you learn to see them as parts of Christ's body instead of ladder climbers, and you ease the burden of loneliness that the ladder creates. You learn to revel also in the gifts of others.

When you throw away your ladder, you realize that Vince Lombardi was only wrong by a few letters: Winning isn't the only thing. It's a lonely thing.

When you stop clutching the ladder, your hands are free— free to hold the hands of other members of the body.

13

Sharing the Gift

In *Hide or Seek* James Dobson observed, "When the birth of a first-born child is imminent his parents pray that he will be normal—that is, 'average.' But from that moment on, average will not be good enough."

When we live in terror of mediocrity, we don't want our children to be mediocre either. We ladder-climbing people are demanding of our families. We force them to join us on the ladder.

Doris is a do-it-all person who takes great pains and gives them to others, especially her husband and children. She is a faucet of advice, instruction, and criticism: Don't forget to. . . . Remember to. . . . Comb your hair before you leave. . . . You mean you forgot to. . . . How on earth could you ever have? . . . Did you remember. . . . Can't you ever. . . . You never. . . .

Her attitude toward herself pours forth in a steady stream toward her family. They alternate wilting, rebelling, and tuning her out.

Doris may have a ladder concept of life, but she isn't competing with her family. She's using them in the competition. They have become her chess pieces in the game of life.

Their achievement is the measure of her worth as a wife and mother. Her husband's promotion is also hers. If her children are attractive, behave properly, and do well in school, she has risen on the ladder. They are extensions of her identity.

She may also be using them, not as extensions, but as replacements. They are going to achieve what she couldn't. They will take her place as achievers in the world. They will be her substitutes. She nags and gives orders—and forgets to praise and enjoy.

She may even see her children as her means of grace, like Wim Pietenpol in James Schaap's moving novel *Home Free*. At 30, Wim's son, Hank, visited his parents' Wisconsin home on furlough from his Central American missionary work. His father was, as always, a faucet of criticism and orders. Hank was, as always, puzzled, hurt, angry. On this visit, though, he learned a reason for his father's attitude.

He knew his parents had waited 20 years for his birth, but he only later discovered they viewed their infertility as punishment from God. When Hank was born, they had said, "This child is special. This child belongs to the Lord." They dedicated him to mission service.

Hank confronted his father: "It's clear now—do you see what it's done to you and me? You never thought of me as a boy, never. I was always like some tiny congregation waiting for a sermon. I mean, you wanted me to be some gift of grace, some barely physical answer to prayer. So all my life, even today, you treat me as if I am simply a soul, some odd, pale physical essence, something to yell at, something to offer to God. I'm special. All my life I've been special. You gave me to God—sure you did, but you never once asked me if that's where I wanted to go. Choice was an unaffordable luxury, wasn't it? It would have been a gamble, because to lose me would be to lose your own forgiveness. You spent your whole life making me perfect, as if your preaching could sanctify me and you at the same time."

We might not promise our children for missionary service,

but we excellence-seekers, like Wim, sometimes treat them as if they were our road to sanctification. They will achieve what we couldn't. We want them to be intelligent, attractive, and to achieve power and status. We want them to become our salvation.

Like Doris, Sue is also a faucet of criticism with her family. Her criticism is filled with running resentment. She is convinced her family is an obstacle to her self-realization.

She thinks, "I could have gone out and made something of myself in the world. I could have had a career as a singer. I was soloist for college choir. But Joe expected me to be home with the children, and so my chances for that were ruined."

In actual fact, she may not be all that sure she could have made a career in singing, and is not all that sure she wanted to, because she, too, feels the tug of the responsibilities of motherhood. But, unable to deal with that ambivalence, one part of herself is projected onto her husband.

Projection may occur with something as simple as leaving home at night. If a woman has mixed feelings about evenings at home with her children and her need for a break from them, she may project half of this ambivalence onto her spouse, handing him the role of never wanting to go out at night and then scapegoating him for their evenings home, when she actually has mixed feelings about leaving the house herself. Some psychologists refer to this process as splitting: separating off an undesirable part of yourself and assigning it to someone else.

Splitting may occur, I think, when we have a contradictory vision of excellence. If, for example, we have a vision of ourselves as both supermom and career-achiever and we haven't been able to resolve that conflict, we may assign responsibility for one of the views to our spouse: "I'd have a career if it weren't for his old-fashioned attitude." Or: "I could stay home with our children if he earned more money."

Sometimes we assign a spouse a role because we like the complementary one. And then we continue to complain about the role they play. The totally responsible woman, who complains about her husband's carefree attitude, may actually want him to remain happy-go-lucky so that she can continue to play the responsible role. And, although he may complain about her nagging to his friends, he may actually like being free to play the eternal adolescent. The workaholic mother who complains about her children not taking household responsibilities may fail to enforce those duties because she has a need to feel overworked.

Carefully test yourself when you start making accusations of *always* and *never* to your spouse. You may have handed him the role to free yourself from your own mixed feelings or to free yourself for the complementary role.

For 15 years Joan had been a long-suffering, heroic wife of an abusive alcoholic. She reentered school, completed a nursing degree, and provided family income. Her church was sympathetic and supportive, listening compassionately to her tell of Steve's drunken bouts and money wasting.

Then, following a near-fatal auto accident, Steve experienced a dramatic conversion. He stopped drinking and began the process of reconstructing his health and his life.

Church members expected Joan to be ecstatic. She wasn't. During his rehabilitation she told them of the unbearable burden of keeping him on his exercise program. The program was reassigned to the supervision of a physical therapist. But the next Sunday she had a new burden: she found it difficult to stay home with him nonstop as she said he needed. A friend volunteered to stay with him a few hours. But when the friend visited, she stayed home, too.

Joan had lost her complementary role as a do-it-all martyr and was trying frantically to regain it.

Whether we treat our families as extensions, replacements, or projections, in our pursuit of excellence, three distortions occur in our relationship with them: 1) our love becomes conditional, 2) we treat them as objects instead of people, and 3) the boundaries of our selves become blurred.

Conditional love, firstly, is love with an "if" attached. It says, "I will love you if you measure up, if you fulfill my expectations." But this love is not scriptural love. God's love for us is *un*conditional. It is love—regardless. And our Lord asks us to love as he loved us—to love regardless of failures, shortcomings, or sins. By his grace our families are good enough for our love just as they are. Love is not earned.

Very few parents have exceptional children, and accepting that frees us to love our children as they are, not as we are sure they ought to be.

June's first child was a bright, early learner. Her second fell behind the charted norms for early childhood development. She recalls, "When my second daughter was four, I panicked. I drilled colors and counting, constantly testing to see if she had mastered them yet. Looking back, I see what incredible pressure I subjected her to. With my oldest I had a sense of play and joy: after all, she was ahead of schedule. But I placed constant pressure on Theresa, and I still see the effects of that on her today."

But slowly June is finding a different attitude emerging toward her second daughter. "When I accept her as she is, when I realize both she and I are good enough, and I know God has a place for each of us, then the sense of joy returns. Then I can help her with schoolwork without the pressure of my standard of excellence."

Secondly, unconditional love acknowledges others as independent persons, not objects. Our first son Chad entered the world a screaming, chunky 10-pounder. When my husband, in his hospital gown and cap, held him for the first time, he looked up at me and said with a mixture of laughter and worry, "What if he turns out to be a 300-pound wrestler?" We had envisioned a child who would share our love of music and language. Confronted with our son in the flesh, we suddenly realized his independent humanity.

John McKay, University of Southern California football coach, was interviewed on TV about his son John's athletic ability. (John was a successful player on his dad's team.) McKay said, "Yes, I'm pleased that John had a good season last year. He does a fine job and I am proud of him. But I would be just as proud if he had never played the game at all."

We excellence-seeking parents can learn a lesson from Coach McKay. We can be just as proud of our children if they never fulfill our parental fantasies at all. To expect that is to treat our children as objects.

There may be a relationship between parents' excellence fantasies and the fact that excellence in education has become such a buzzword. Our excellence drive is especially strong regarding our children.

In the third distortion that occurs when we treat our families as extensions of ourselves, we blur the boundaries of self. Marilyn's 11-year-old daughter Angie is a competition swimmer. Before several swim meets Marilyn gave Angie lots of advice about getting along with the team members. She made sure she bought a stylish swimsuit and suggested several games for Angie to take along to play with team members when she wasn't competing.

At a swim meet she saw Angie sitting playing one of the games by herself. She said, "It didn't seem to bother Angie, but it pierced my heart. I went to my seat on the bleachers asking myself why it was so painful for me to see her alone and so important to me that she be accepted. Then I looked around on the bleachers and realized that I didn't feel accepted by the other swimmers' parents. I didn't feel part of them. I was taking my personal battle and handing it to Angie."

Marilyn had blurred her boundaries. She had assigned her own issues to her daughter's life. In both marriage and parenting a sense of our own boundaries is necessary. Marriage is a partnership of two independent human beings, not a total merger. Spouses and parents need a sense of self, a knowledge of their own boundaries in treating their families as persons and loving them unconditionally.

Perhaps a good first step in freeing our families from the

burden of our excellence drive is to test our expectations of our love relationships. Many of us excellence-seekers have unrealistic shoulds for our close relationships.

Ask yourself: Do I expect myself to be a perfect spouse? Do I expect marriage to be continual romance? Do I feel compelled to protect my children from failure? Do I blame myself for their shortcomings?

Review the processes of challenging your shoulds from Chapter 6, and uncover your automatic thoughts during disturbing events in your family life. Identify those vague, free-floating dissatisfactions. Challenge those shoulds that have a wrong purpose, give you false responsibility, or are outdated.

Then, stop playing superspouse, supermom, or superdad. Just be your good-enough self, redeemed by grace. And as that good-enough spouse and parent you may want to make the following choices.

The choice of balance

Teach your children about balance instead of best. Teach them: "Give the job the time it deserves" instead of "Always do your best." As Marilyn grows in knowing she is good enough, she learns not to pressure Angie as much. "The best swimmer on Angie's team does well at state meets," said Marilyn. "But then, she's had private lessons since kindergarten, and after school her parents are often at the pool with her, giving her further instruction. At nine she attended out-of-town meets without her parents—and cried herself to sleep because she was homesick.

"We don't want to put that much pressure on Angie. We want more balance in her life, and we tell her that." (For more on balance, see Chapter 16.)

The choice of positive reinforcement

Spouses and children need family members who see the half-full glass, not the half empty one. My three-year-old son made a mistake when he pointed to a toy clock and said to a visiting friend, "I got this for a birthday present. Someone gave it to me." It had been a Christmas present, not a birthday present.

My first impulse was to say, "No, Matt, a Christmas present, not a birthday present." But I closed my lips on the correction. He had just formed two grammatically correct sentences. He had retrieved information which was eight months old. He was making social conversation with a child his age at snack time and talking with his mouth empty. Why should I rush in to correct the one tiny flaw?

I admit, though, that I couldn't totally resist. After a few seconds I said, "Yes, Matt, it was a present. Grandpa and Grandma gave it to you last Christmas, remember?"

Seeing the half-full glass doesn't mean insincere, extravagant praise. It doesn't mean avoiding all correction. It simply means enjoying with them the pleasure of a task. It means saying, "I like the color combination in that painting." It means, "You printed your name neatly. I like that." It means, "The yard looks nice after you mowed and watered it."

The choice of hilarity

In the Middle Ages, the church listed *hilaritas* (the Latin root for hilarity) among the minor virtues. *Hilaritas* refers to a joyful confidence, to saying yes to life, even when faced with difficulties. Rev. Robert Meyering's challenge of hilarity has stayed with me as a principle of family life in the year and a half since I first read it. He wrote, "The challenge of parenting is to be able to step back every now and then and realize with a smile in your heart that you don't own these children, that you don't own your spouse, that you don't even own yourself. You are owned . . .

"Be at peace with yourself. Remember that God made our children: They are forever and indelibly marked by the good Lord. In a world already full of advice for good and successful parenting, here's another piece of advice: Enjoy your children, and let them grow. Let them develop their own peculiar quirks and twists. They will anyway. So you might as well smile occasionally and enjoy the process" ("Hilarity: More than a Minor Virtue," *Christian Home and School,* May/June 1986).

Practice hilarity: the joyful confidence of knowing you and your family are owned.

The choice of sharing the gift

Since worth is God's free gift, your family's failures don't affect their worth or yours. Knowing this and living this allows you to separate the sin from the sinner, to divide the event and the person. When your son flunks spelling, his personal worth does not plunge. When your husband loses his job, he still has value.

Penalizing a child for her misbehavior doesn't demean her, it simply forces her to face the consequences of her actions. It doesn't mean the loss of your love or your respect.

James Dobson believes it is easy to convey love and disrespect at the same time. He says, "A child can know that you would actually give your life for him if required, and yet your doubts about his acceptability show through. You are tense and nervous when he starts to speak to guests or outsiders. You butt in to explain what he was trying to say or laugh nervously when his remarks sound foolish. . . . You reveal your frustration when you are trying to comb his hair or make him 'look nice' for an important event. He knows you think it is an impossible assignment. . . . Loving your child, therefore is only half of the task of building self-esteem. . . . Unless *somebody* believes in his worth, the world can be a cold and lonely place, indeed."

Recognizing our family members' worth and granting them that respect, you acknowledge that in Christ, with you, they have worth. You share the gift of good enough.

Knowing and sharing the gift of good enough is the first

step of two. It's accepting our inability to do it all. One question remains. What, then, am I to do? How do I find my personal tasks in God's world? The next four chapters provide suggestions to help find answers to this second question. They help in deciding what to do.

14

Finding Your Calling

Karen, in the late 1960s, was a warm but flighty college coed. We both left college, and she dropped from my life for 15 years. Then, on a vacation trip, I met her after a worship service at her church.

I asked about her life. "I'm teaching first grade," she said, resting her hand on the shoulder of her 10-year-old son Eric. "I love it." She tousled his hair and he grinned at her. "I've found my niche," she said.

On my way back to the car I compared the woman to the coed. It was as if she'd turned on a gyrocompass, that device that always points true north. Still the same warm Karen, but she had lost her flighty lack of direction. She had found her niche.

Finding our calling is to turn on our gyrocompasses and know direction in our lives. Finding our calling is to find work we can do, knowing we are good enough.

Asking the question of calling eases the anxiety and paralysis of the excellence question. Finding our calling is to stop asking the question, "How well?" and to ask instead the question, "What task?"

Last year when a publisher asked me to complete an article

on a very tight schedule, I consented—and immediately pan-icked. "Can I do it?" I wondered. "Can I create the article on such a short deadline? Will it be good enough?"

Paralysis set in. Anxiety reigned. For three days I couldn't produce a word. I prayed, "Lord, if this is a task you have for me, then lead where I should go. It's your work, and I am your daughter, here to serve. Lead me in ways that will honor you and your way with the world." When I prayed that prayer of calling, I could move forward again. Paralysis and anxiety were eased.

In Chapter 5 we looked at the general calling of all good-enough people. We saw our task of glorifying God and enjoying him forever. We examined the general assignment of loving God above all and our neighbor as ourselves.

The calling to God is primary for each good-enough per-son. Each is called, first of all to a person: Jesus Christ. He leads us out of the jungle of our own pride. That primary calling to our Lord never changes.

Os Guinness says that calling should never be reduced to a place or a thing. My calling is never simply to Africa or Iowa. My calling is never only to law, medicine, or parenthood. My calling is first of all to my creator-redeemer.

Within that primary calling each of us has a secondary calling, and it may take many forms. Each of us has a unique place for work in God's plan. That's a miracle of a good-enough life. Our master knows each of us by name and has a place for each of us.

When we seek our place, we realize our limits. We know that God is infinite and in charge, and we are simply finding our assignment. Os Guinness compares one's calling to a bull's eye, surrounded by concentric circles. We are at the center of our bull's eye, and our responsibility gradually diminishes with each succeeding concentric circle. God alone sees the whole picture.

Pastor Jerry Hoek of Cedar Rapids, Iowa, learned an ob-ject lesson in the limits of our calling when his three-year-old wanted to help him put together a 2000-piece puzzle. His son had helped with a couple of pieces, and on the day Jerry completed the puzzle his son burst into sobs. He had wanted to help finish. So Jerry took apart a few pieces, put his son on his lap, and together they finished the puzzle.

Reflecting on the incident, Jerry saw a parallel in God's nurturing his children: "He wants us to do what we can and put whatever pieces of the puzzle together we can. We certainly cannot do the whole thing for we cannot even see the whole picture. But we can see small parts of it, and it is those parts that God says we can help with." What a privilege to sit on our Father's lap and put in a few pieces of the puzzle!

Although our primary calling remains the same, our secondary callings may change. We are called to parenting, and our children grow up. We are called to marriage, and our spouse dies. We are called to bookkeeping, and the firm closes. In today's fast-changing culture it is likely that a working person will change careers at least once in a lifetime.

We are more equipped to weather those shifts in secondary callings if our primary calling is secure. That doesn't mean that we weather them painlessly, but it does mean that we still have our gyrocompasses. We can go back to the master and ask, "Now what? That task seems to be over. What's next?"

We recognize that we are servants, not the master. We are the children, not the Father. We can be called by the master instead of driven by excellence. We can be still and know that he is God.

Throughout the history of Christendom the meaning of calling has gone through shifts of emphasis. In medieval times, calling was seen as belonging to the spiritual, otherworldly realm. To be called was to dedicate yourself to prayer and fasting, withdraw from the world, take a vow of chastity, and spend your days meditating. To find your calling was to spend some time every hour in the chapel.

Luther and the other reformers challenged this narrowing of the meaning of calling and restored dignity to vocations.

They rediscovered that we need not renounce the world and head for a monastery to serve the Lord. They saw again that this is our Father's world. Any form of work can be done as to the Lord. They rediscovered the second half of our task: to love our neighbor as ourself.

But in evolving a "Protestant work ethic" our world has gone a step further than the reformers. We have once again narrowed the meaning of calling, this time restricting it to occupation. We sometimes equate work-for-pay and calling. We have lost the broader view of our work in God's world and made an idol of careers.

When Scripture talks of calling (vocation), it doesn't mean simply the work-for-pay done by believers. For Scripture and for the reformers calling was broader than occupation. It means our calling to be children of God. It means our entire life. It means all of the tasks a believer finds to do in life, each of his or her hats and roles: parent, church member, citizen, spouse. Each of these hats is part of our calling on this earth.

The narrowing of the meaning of calling has resulted in a low status being assigned to nonpaying work such as home-making, childrearing, and volunteer services. If we limit calling to paying occupations, we have denied meaning to more than half the population. We have eliminated all children, home-makers, the jobless, volunteer workers, retired people, and the homebound from the possibility of calling.

Calling is not limited to a career! Calling is our reasonable service to God in whatever phase of life we find ourself. It includes our whole selves and our entire lives.

When our career is closely linked with the core of our identity, we are blessed. But in this fallen world that blessing does not always happen. The apostle Paul's occupation was tent making, and it was part of his calling by God. But his work as apostle to the Gentiles was more crucial to his sense of identity, closer to his core, to his heart.

In our fractured world farmers may be forced into day labor to support their families when a sour farm economy forces them into bankruptcy. Women may return to the work force in slots which are not challenging because they've missed job training in order to rear their children. Students may train for teaching, engineering, or business management, and find few job openings in their chosen fields.

For such persons, as well as those not in jobs-for-pay, it is comforting to remember that calling does not equal career. In this fallen world, occupation is not always a perfect match with skills and gifts. A shift in future conditions may result in a better match, and it may not. But either way, such a person is still called as a child of God to work in his world. Keeping our primary call in focus, as well as the broader nature of calling, can help to keep such disappointments from turning into bitterness.

We need to remind ourselves that God sees us as good enough, and that we still have tasks to pursue. To follow our calling is to seek first the kingdom of God and his righteousness.

But how do we find our secondary calling? In my life, God doesn't very often zap me with lightning bolts of blinding revelation. I don't wake up each morning to find that God has written an agenda for the day on my daily planner. God deals with us as people, not pawns. We are sons and daughters, not slaves. We are loved—but that doesn't mean he makes every move for us.

So we make choices. And we make them daily, weekly, yearly. We ask, "Lord, guide me in my choices for this day, this week, this year." Then we make choices in our secondary calling. Finding our calling is an interactive process in which we are God's partners.

However, making choices as God's partners still leaves us with the question, "If God doesn't zap me with lightning or write my daily agenda or 10-year-plan, what guidelines do I use in finding and pursuing my calling? How do I recognize my tasks?"

At 28 Mary asked the question of calling. She had dropped

out of college at 18 to marry. Now a widow and mother of three, she sought new direction for her life. Haunted by the Bible verse, "Without vision, the people perish," she felt a need for vision. She explored work and training options. An old friend said, "Mary, you were always a super student. Why not go back to school?"

"With three kids, how probable is that?" Mary asked.

"About as probable as you'd like to make it," her friend answered.

The next day she visited the local college to check into programs. At 28 she returned to school with a goal of becoming a teacher-counselor. Mary had become an informal counselor for several Christian single friends. She felt her lack of training, but also sensed her skills.

"My knees knocked that first day back on campus," she said. "But when I went to convocation, it was as if I heard God say to me, 'You're where I want you to be for this new chapter of your life.' My eyes filled with tears."

Not all callings are as dramatic as Mary's, but the guidelines for her decision are universal. Mary used her gifts and interests, the world's need, her opportunities, and the still small voice.

Gifts and interest

Our gifts are our abilities which have developed from our heredity and our environment. Each of us has different aptitudes and skills which are a factor to consider in seeking our calling. Given a good mind, a strong compassion, a knack for numbers, or a way with children, we consider those gifts in making our choices.

Sometimes the Lord prepares us with skills we don't realize we will need. When I was in college I added an extra minor—German—simply because I enjoyed twisting my tongue through its gutteral and trilled sounds, and because I liked the challenge. I planned to teach high school English and speech. But two years later I was offered a college teaching assistant position that required teaching a beginning German course while a professor completed his doctoral work.

The way of God with his children is not one of waste. The parable of the talents teaches us that. Although the parable is about money, it has wider application, too. But the parable of the talents can be misused as a guilt trap. The talents were areas of responsibility, not just potentials. We must not misuse the parable to flog ourselves for not developing every single potential we have.

Because of the limits of time and responsibility, each of us has potentials we will never use in this life. The talents were assigned responsibilities. Every potential I have is not a responsibility, although some potentials may be. Potential needs to be considered in balance with other items. Two people may have the same natural aptitude for calculus, but the engineer has more calling to develop that aptitude than the lawyer.

Closely related to our gifts are our interests. One student I know was afraid she was being called to Africa as a missionary, although her tolerance for heat and bugs was very low. She was relieved when her pastor told her that God often uses our gifts and interests as guides in our calling.

The world's need

Our gifts and interests are counterbalanced sometimes by a third guideline: our knowledge of need. Dr. Peter Boelens, administrator for the Luke Society, made a need-based decision. Working as a medical doctor for that ministry of medical mercy to the world's poor, he was asked to become its administrator. At first he refused the offer. His interests and aptitudes were medicine, not administration. Then he changed his mind. The job needed doing, and he knew he was best qualified to do it. He says with a wry smile, "Now I make it possible for others to do the work I love." But he does it with joy, not bitterness. He's turned on his gyrocompass!

Need may rule when a sick friend needs someone to care for her children for a week, and you're not by nature good at coping with extra stress. Need may outweigh gifts. Need outweighed gifts when I played a rusty accompaniment for the singing of the senior citizen's group.

Opportunities

A fourth consideration in calling is opportunity. Rena is a bright, 60-year-old woman with a master's degree in chemistry, who has used her degree in both teaching and industry. At Bible study one evening when the subject of calling arose, she said a trifle wistfully, "When I was in college, I planned to become a medical doctor, but at that time medical schools weren't accepting women." She wondered briefly what would have happened in her life if she'd been born half a century later. But then she returned again to her normal, optimistic self. Her sense of calling was altered by her situation, and she has accepted that. She may work to bring about a more just system for other women and rejoices in their opportunities. But she found a sense of calling despite an unjust culture.

If you would like a teaching position in your current location and none is available, you will need to reconsider your calling. If you would like to rear a daughter and God sends you only sons, your calling is limited by their biology.

The still, small voice

A fifth consideration in leading us in our calling is the still, small voice, a knowledge that surpasses reason. It may be a sense of continual tugging in a certain direction. It may be a quiet certainty that pervades during prayer or Bible reading.

Os Guinness tells students (and strugglers with midlife crises) to pray about their calling daily for six months, to discuss their self-concept with friends, to study the options earnestly, and they may come to a deep sense of who they are that goes beyond words. It is not something, he said, that you can just spit out in 10 words at a moment's notice. It goes beyond words. Life is, as author John Claypool said, not a problem to be solved, but a mystery to be lived.

This mystical sense of calling needs a groundwork of prayer and worship—both public and private. It needs the groundwork of living close to God's Word. It requires a body of believers.

That sense of certainty is not continuous, and it is not always equally strong. This morning as I sit at my word processor in the 5:30 A.M. stillness, I am at peace with my current calling to be a writer of words, a mother of three sons, a wife. . . . But yesterday with the repairman stepping around seven mounds of laundry, my three sons whining for snacks, and an editor on the telephone, my assurance faded.

Sometimes, when we do not see our way clearly, we simply take the leap of faith. Having looked at our gifts, our interests, the need, and our opportunities, and hearing no still, small voice, we simply make the choice because it is required, and required now. Because we still see through a glass darkly, our leaps may sometimes be a process of trial and error.

Using these five guidelines, we may decide we are on track in our current tasks. Asking the excellence questions, we may have stumbled upon our calling unawares—and we will keep doing what we have been doing, simply realizing that our tasks are our service to God, not a measure of our worth. Or we may do as Ray did. At 40, he left his bakery to retrain for a job teaching high school English.

Asking the question of calling, though, is fundamentally different from asking the excellence question. We are simply collaborating with God. We are putting in our few puzzle pieces by his gracious permission. We are not on a continual quest for first place, success, growth, or perfection.

Preparing breakfast each morning doesn't bring me any closer to any of those four excellence goals, but it is part of my current calling. Teaching preschool may not make you rich, but it may be your task. You may not be the country's number one organist, but you may be called to provide music for your church's worship. You may not be a perfect mother, but you may be called to rear children.

To find our calling is to live in the present with our real self, not in the mythical future with our ideal self. To find our calling is to find a sense of purpose which makes our short-comings pale in comparison. That was Golda Meir's experience. She said, looking back, "I was never a beauty. There was a time when I was sorry about that, when I was old enough to understand the importance of it and, looking into the mirror, realized it was something I was never going to have. . . . I found what I wanted to do in life, and being pretty no longer had any importance" (*Confidence*, Augsburg, 1987).

Like Golda in political leadership and Karen in teaching first grade, we can find our niche. Or like Mary and Ray, we can find a series of niches for different life stages. We can turn on the gyrocompass of calling and stay on course glorifying and enjoying God. We can find—and go on finding—our calling.

15

Setting Your Goals

The *decision* to go after a goal is the key to success," says one Christian writer. "As you pursue excellence, you will find that the world around you will have an almost uncanny way of stepping aside when you say, 'This is my goal. I am going to reach it.'"

What powerful concepts! What powerful words! When I read these words—and words like them—in motivational literature, I find myself with an automatic response. I become a sort of Pavlovian dog. I become excited. I drool!

"Just think of the power I'd have if I could only set my goals and head for them," I think. "The world could be mine. It would step aside. I'd soar to new heights, find new skills, fit more into my schedule. I'd know where I was headed."

After reading a book on the need for goals, I sat down one morning and wrote out goals, just wrote them down as they came to me. They filled two pages. As instructed, I wrote my lifetime goals, my five-year goals, and how I would spend my time if I had only six months to live. Then, as the book advised, I picked three of them and wrote a page on how I could achieve those goals. Then I began writing a schedule for my daily routine. Nine pages in all. The schedule in that notebook has three entries, one for 7:00, 7:30, and 8:30. The rest of the page is blank.

I don't recall referring to those pages again after the day I wrote them. They are dated January 19, 1976.

The fever of going for the gold passed, and they disappeared into my files. I stumbled across them in researching relics from my past for writing this book. I had read the material on goals, feverishly decided goals were the solution to my life's needs, and in a burst of enthusiasm wrote them out.

I suspect that burst of enthusiasm happens to other excellence seekers when they read material suggesting we go for the goal and the gold.

Have you tried writing goals? Perhaps, after your initial burst of enthusiasm, you have done as I did: I didn't write any goals for the next decade.

In 1976, after reading about goal setting, I was convinced: 1) that I currently had no goals, and 2) that setting goals would solve my life's problems. Neither conviction was true.

I see, looking back over the past decade, that I already had goals when I sat down to write those nine pages of material. I wasn't creating goals. I was simply putting on paper the drives that I had not previously articulated or formalized. I see as I read over those lists from the mists of my past that many of those same drives and directions are still with me, even though I never looked at those pages again.

I think of Kathryn whom I used to consider a goal-less person because she flits from task to task. But as I get to know Kathryn better, I realize she is not without goals. On the contrary, she has too many of them: keep up correspondence with all of her friends and relatives, keep her home meticulously clean, plan social events for the lonely people in the church, learn to play violin. She flits from goal to shining goal with little forward movement toward any of them, lamenting her lack of progress and not understanding the reasons.

Setting goals does not mean creating goals from a void.

Setting goals means formalizing and clarifying the goals which we have, but are not aware of. As creatures moving through time, we are headed in a direction: we have goals, either conscious or subconscious. Even people locked into a life of compulsive ritual have a goal of maintaining the status quo against the forces of change.

By clarifying our goals, we see the tug-of-war between conflicting directions we sometimes set for ourselves. We see the need to make choices. We may need to choose between being a home-schooling supermom and reentering the work force when our children reach school age.

Setting goals may mean solidifying goals which are effervescent and fragmented. We may vacillate between parenting that is authoritarian and parenting that is permissive, seeing ourselves one day as firm-handed and the next as gentle and understanding. We may picture ourselves as khaki-clad outdoor hikers one day and as delicate indoor needleworkers the next.

Setting goals also means setting limits so that our goals are within the realm of possibility. As we have seen in previous chapters, our excellence goal, unarticulated, may be to play God. We may want to be all-knowing and all-powerful.

Setting goals does not mean inventing them, but it may mean narrowing, broadening, clarifying, solidifying, shrinking, or eliminating goals which already exist undeclared in our lives.

The second myth I accepted in 1976 was that goals would revolutionize my life and clear up my difficulties. I would be successful and the world would step aside. I was going for my goal! Achieving my goals would make me feel good enough. Heading for my goals would give my life meaning. Achieving them would give me a sense of worth.

I gave goals too much credit. I gave goals the credit that belongs to grace alone. As we have seen in earlier chapters, worth and the sense of good enough are gift, all gift, and achieving goals is not going to provide that for us. Goals are only a result of our sense of direction and purpose. We can set goals if we have a sense of our calling. They can be a way of providing structure for that calling.

Goals are a sort of skeleton, a bone structure for living. They are not the entire body of life. They aren't the surging blood of joy or the muscle of effort, but simply the skeleton that gives it shape. When goals are everything to us, we become walking skeletons. Joy evaporates. We no longer take time for play. Worship loses meaning.

If we think goals are created from nothing and that they will solve all of life's problems, we may write nine pages of material and try desperately to live out those pages, or we may give up. If, however, we understand the limitations of goals, they can be useful tools for life—not life itself, but tools.

We can more easily pass the hurdle of procrastinating our goal setting if we realize we already have goals, but they may need some adjustments. We dare to set goals if we don't expect them to provide instant contentment or worth.

A good-enough-through-Christ goal setter remembers several important principles in clarifying goals.

1. Good-enough goal-setters leave open a window.

Houa Yang, a 21-year-old Laotian refugee attending Bible College, translated several Christian creeds into a Laotian language and distributed his work among fellow Laotian refugees. Interviewing him for a Christian magazine, I asked about his plans for the future. "I don't set goals," he answered gently, "I try to be open to the leading of the Lord."

Having said that, he added that he planned to continue attending Bible college and was considering becoming a missionary among Laotians in the United States.

Houa Yang was leaving open a window as he planned his life. He set a direction for the future but also stayed open to a change of course by the Lord.

His attitude is in stark contrast to the secular mindset which says, "I am the captain of my fate and the master of my destiny."

We set goals as stewards, not as kings and queens. We set goals, realizing they may be overruled. That's the meaning of Thomas à Kempis's adage, "Man proposes, but God disposes."

James Dobson learned to leave open a window when working on his book *Hide or Seek*, which he was finding hard to shape. His father read it and, for the first time ever, yawned over his son's material. His wife told him something was wrong, but she couldn't put her finger on it.

Dobson remembers, "Finally I turned to Shirley and said, 'I know the message of this book is needed by parents and their children. They are hurting and I can help. Maybe God doesn't want me to write it for some reason.'

'Then what do you intend to do?' she asked.

'I'm going to spend one more day on this book. Only *one*! I plan to attack the entire manuscript with a pair of scissors tomorrow morning. Nothing I've written will be safe from deletion or rearrangement. I also plan to fast tomorrow (going without food in an atmosphere of prayer and dependence on God). Then if I still feel defeated by tomorrow night, I will throw away what I've written and go home.' "

The next morning after prayer, he attacked the manuscript. He says, "Every piece fell together like a jigsaw puzzle, as though the Great Designer were guiding my efforts."

Dobson concludes, "It is now obvious that God permitted me to go through that period of self-doubt for a purpose. . . . You see I had begun to depend on myself, instead of being an instrument of His purposes and plan. I believe he wanted me to understand that my 'ministry' to families is not my own, but is managed by his own hand. I responded by giving my meager talent back to the Source whence it came originally."

James Dobson learned how to keep open a window. And through that window he saw the reason for a goal unreached.

We don't always see the reason. When our second son turned three, Marlo and I planned for a third child to complete our family. Our plans crashed in searing pain when Craig was stillborn.

I didn't understand. I still don't. But I learned with empty arms that I was a steward, not the master.

Our task became working through grief instead of caring for a newborn. As we grieved, we asked about our future and our family. A year and a half later our son Matthew was born. I still don't know God's reasons for allowing Craig's death, but I have accepted that window. I am a servant-daughter, not a queen.

2. Good-enough goal-setters set goals to match their task.

When my pastor asked me to write a two-page summary of our church's past and present for a local history book, I groaned. I pictured digging through two decades of church bulletins for interesting tidbits. I thought of the effort (and imagination) that would be required to make it captivating. I estimated a couple weeks of work.

I wasn't willing to contribute two weeks of my writing time. But, rethinking the project, I realized I hadn't set an appropriate goal. I could work for two years and my two-page church history still would not be a riveting piece of drama.

So I set a different goal: two pages of concise information that captured the flow of my church's history clearly and concretely. Instead of going through mountains of church bulletins, I asked my pastor for information. "Check the church anniversary books," he said. I made a stop at the church library for the annuals and anniversary books. I made three phone calls to gather current data. I spent an hour or two organizing, rewriting, and editing the material in the annuals, added the current data, and the job was done. It was adequate for its purpose: providing information about my congregation for the local history book. It was not brilliant, not dramatic, but good enough for its task. My goal had become reasonable and appropriate.

Sometimes others can help us shape appropriate goals. Recovering perfectionist Dorothy gives her goals to her husband for feedback in order to double-check them. She says,

"He knows how I can overextend myself, and he can tell when the list is too ambitious. He's a good set of brakes if I've made my list for the month too long."

In setting goals, we remember our primary calling to God. We keep in mind our secondary calling—found through our gifts, interests, opportunities, the need, and the inner voice. On this foundation we set goals. Good-enough goal setting builds on calling.

With a sense of calling you recognize the myth quality to the unlimited potential in setting your goals. You realize the need to make choices. You abandon a goal list which includes: Keep the house in perfect order. Keep the car looking and running like brand new. Find (or continue) an exciting career. Home school my children. Volunteer for hospice. Teach Sunday school. Run for city council. You set, instead, goals which are appropriate for your calling and task.

3. Good-enough goal-setters remember TTT.

Closely related to appropriate and reasonable goals is the TTT concept. I learned the TTT principle from Piet Hein's poem, which I like so well I've memorized it.

> Put up in a place
> Where it's easy to see
> The cryptic admonishment
> T.T.T.
>
> When you feel how depressingly
> Slowly you climb,
> It's well to remember that
> Things Take Time.

Like it? You may want to memorize it, too. Then recite it often!

4. Good-enough goal-setters know that a straight line may not be the shortest distance to a goal.

Writer Ron Klug says that in order to write better he first

has to write worse. He has to simply shut off his critical editor self for a while and let his creative self produce without critique. His wife, Lyn, also a writer, has learned the same lesson. Working hard to write well for a book of devotions for women, she found herself producing gnarled and difficult reading. The harder she tried, the more convoluted her sentences became. She packed a suitcase, left for a retreat house with one goal: produce 10 devotionals per day, not worrying about the quality. She did that—and as the week went on, her writing got better and better. The shortest distance to good writing was not a straight line.

People who have epiphanies of discovery have also learned the value of giving up the goal. Have you ever tried frantically to remember a name, given up, and then had it flash to mind when you were working on another task? The shortest distance to remembering was not the straight line of trying relentlessly.

My goal is to finish drafting this chapter by tomorrow evening. As I type, my three-year-old son Matthew plays with Legos beside my desk. Half an hour ago he nagged and whined and said he couldn't get them together right. I put him off with several quick suggestions and kept typing.

But after three unhappy interruptions, I left my chair and spent 10 minutes building Lego airplanes with him. He's flying those airplanes through an imaginary sky, and I've returned to my desk. The shortest distance to this draft was not a straight line!

5. Good-enough goal-setters realize that failure to achieve their goals doesn't forfeit their gift of good enough.

Gloria says, "I set goals, and sometimes I fail to reach them. Then I see myself as a failure in God's eyes." She lowers her goals, and feels guilty about lowering them.

Gloria has forgotten the gift of good enough. In her goals and guilt she ignores grace.

Failure to reach goals doesn't forfeit grace! If at this point you feel a need for expansion of this principle, simply go back and read Chapter 4. Remind yourself that being good enough is a gift, not a goal achieved.

So much for principles. What about practicalities? How can a good-enough person take steps in goal setting?

Perhaps a place to begin is to state what your goals are not. Gather together some of those unreasonable shoulds you've eliminated, add a few characteristics of your ideal self in the mythical future, and write a list of nongoals. My goal is not to have everyone like me, to raise geniuses, to live without mistakes, to fulfill all my potentials.

Another useful step may be to set some process, rather than product, goals. Farmers know they don't have ultimate control of their harvest. They plant, they cultivate, they fertilize—but one hailstorm or a summer of drought, and the crop can be lost. They have a measure of control over the process, but not the product.

A physical therapist explained her profession, "One of the difficult things about physical therapy is to remember that I can't force healing to take place. The body has to heal itself. I can only create conditions that allow healing." She does her work using hot and cold packs, ultrasound, and cortisone. She coaxes muscles and joints through the needed range-of-motion, producing conditions for healing. She follows the process without total control of the product.

Reaching the goal is a gift, and failing to reach it is a different gift. But our responsibility is to be faithful in the process.

In *Feeling Good: The New Mood Therapy* Dr. David Burns compared process goals to driving a car. He said he felt like a failure whenever a therapy session with a patient did not go well and a patient gave him the run around or responded negatively. Then his colleague Dr. Beck suggested he imagine he had a job driving a car. Some days he'd hit mostly green lights and make good time. Other days he'd hit lots of red ones, and the trip would take longer. But his driving skill each day was the same. Just aim for good, consistent effort, Beck advised him.

To set process goals is to aim for good, consistent driving.

Another way to get your goals under control, especially if you are a perfectionist who pursues a task *ad infinitum* is to set time limits. This might work for you if your job of straightening the kitchen after breakfast in the morning takes until noon because you end up mopping the floor, cleaning the crevices around your sink with a knife, and reorganizing the cupboard in which you found a butter smear. Time limit goals might help if you are the kind of person for whom reading an evening story to your children turns into reading aloud half a novel. Or if your Christmas card mailing list turns each personal note into a detailed letter. If that is how you tend to operate, you may want to try setting time limit goals for your short-term goals. Today, this week I will spend an hour on _____ , two hours on _____ , three hours on _____ .

The time limit goal is: I will do 15 minutes of vigorous exercise three times this week. It is not: I will be able to do 40 sit-ups by the end of the week. The time limit goal is: I will spend half an hour straightening the house each morning. It is not: I will keep this house spotless. A time limit goal is to spend an hour a week at the piano, not to memorize "Rhapsody in Blue" by the end of the month.

But process goals and time limit goals are not the only kinds of goals. Product goals are useful, too. For product goals you may want to:

1) Keep them short and simple. Instead of filling nine pages, for the past two years I have written my goals on a 3x5-inch card.

2) Write them down. My grandmother, as far as I know, never had a set of written goals in her life. But she had a clear sense of who she was and where she was headed. She lived in a slower-paced and more structured era. Her life on the farm as the mother of 11 children followed a yearly ritual of planting and harvesting. Of preserving meat and vegetables and fruits

for the winter. Of baking enough bread for the week. Of caring for another baby every year or two. And when her children were grown, she filled her life with quilt making, mending the clothes of her 50 grandchildren, and helping her daughters can green beans and applesauce.

My choices are more complex. I need the tool of writing them out to manage.

3) Divide. If you set goals for a longer period of time, break them down into smaller increments. What do you want to do this month, this week, today, to move toward your goal?

4) Review. Goals unreviewed are easily forgotten. It may be helpful to keep your list of goals with your yearly calendar so they are handy for periodic review.

5) Revise. Goals unrevised can become dinosaurs. We can climb a ladder to a goal, only to discover we had our ladder against the wrong wall!

One goal-glorifying speaker I heard told the story of a 15-year-old who set 127 goals for himself. Now an adult, he has reached 107 of these 127 goals. For the first 30 seconds I was impressed. He was a young man with a vision and determination, I thought. Then I thought of my growth during the decades since I was 15. Would I really want to be locked into goals set by myself as a 15-year-old adolescent? No way! I no longer want to be a flight attendant.

Good-enough goal setting includes the right to revise as we develop.

6) Allow a time cushion. Life rarely goes exactly as planned. Good-enough goal setting leaves time for the unexpected: the spilled milk, the dirty shoes, the drop-in visitor. Someone has suggested we rename interruptions divine interventions.

God's most important task for you today may not be on your agenda. Keep that window open by building in a time cushion. If unscheduled time makes you nervous, you can plan an optional activity in the wonderful event that the time cushion becomes unnecessary.

7) Practice balance. Set goals for different areas of your life, not just one. Set goals for your personal, professional, marital, parenting, church, and community roles, as appropriate.

But balance is another chapter. Before we examine balance, let's glance back at goals. Remember: a key is to set reasonable goals in keeping with our calling and to be open to divine interruptions.

Now onward!

16

Keeping a Balance

My women's Bible study group was celebrating the end of our year with a luncheon. As we ate our chicken-and-grape salad and sipped from long-stemmed glasses, our conversation turned to motivating our children.

"Jim can get A's, but he's not interested in school work," said Marilyn. "He'd rather be practicing basketball. In a social studies project students could choose their grade by contract, and he chose B. We tell him, 'Jim, you should always do your best.' "

Each of the eight mothers seated around the perfectly pressed table cloth nodded. We recognized the motto. We'd all said it.

I remembered saying it to my oldest son when he was absorbed in reading *Popular Science* instead of memorizing a map of Palestine. I've said it to my second son when he wanted to give up in his struggle with spelling.

"Always do your best," I said. "Always do your best."

But as I brushed the corner of my mouth with a linen napkin, I thought of the meals I served my family. I certainly don't "do my best" in each meal I serve them. I could serve three-course meals on white table linens, but our family fare falls slightly short of such elegance.

I could also spend more time teaching my preschooler to read and helping him learn more about this wonderful world. My windows will never be totally free of every molecule of dust, even if I clean them three times a day. How can I always do my best?

C. T. Studd—scholar, athlete, heir to a fortune—gave his best to missions. He created a sensation in the 19th century when he dedicated himself to foreign mission service. He worked 18-hour days, seven days per week. He expected the same dedication of his fellow missionaries.

He spent 10 years in China with his family, where his health failed. After recovering in England he worked in India for six years until his health again failed. In 1912 he left England for Africa, in spite of the objections of his sick wife and daughters whom he left in England. He returned to England only once before his death in 1931.

C. T. Studd died a broken man. He had become addicted to morphine. His mission had been convulsed with controversy. He had been removed from the mission he himself had founded. C. T. Studd found his best had destroyed him.

He was destroyed because "best" is a mistaken standard. Life is not first of all a matter of what's best, but a matter of balance. C. T. Studd was driven to best without balance. He identified his mission work as his only area of service to the Lord and neglected the rest of his life. He gave his best, his all, to that job, instead of simply giving the task the time it deserved.

Not all do-it-all people narrow themselves as much as C. T. Studd. In fact, some do just the opposite. Instead of becoming too narrow, they spread themselves too thin. They commit themselves to too many roles and tasks. And they still feel compelled to do their best at each. A focus too broad is just as frustrating as a focus too narrow.

Think for a moment of the dimensions of your personal

life. You spend time on: your biological needs (eating, sleeping, etc.), your appearance, your physical fitness, your faith, your curiosity and intellect, your artistic skills, your emotional well-being.

Broaden your thinking to include your relationships. Think of your responsibility to any of the people or groups listed: children, spouse, parents, other family members, neighbors, friends, people in need, employer, coworkers.

Think of your obligations to institutions and organizations: your home, local church, denomination, children's schools, alma mater, city, state, country, local library, clubs or groups, civic organizations, charitable organizations.

Alvin Toffler calls our predicament one of facing "overchoice." The comic strip character Pogo observed, "Gentlemen, we are surrounded by insurmountable opportunity."

Faced with these multiple choices for roles, Sophie Kerr wrote that it had always been a fancy of hers to live six lives at the same time: "One life for the necessary work of earning my living, . . . One life for reading and study and meditation on what I'd read and what I'd studied. One life for doing things with my hands like sewing and gardening. . . . One life to see my friends and acquaintances. One life for political and public interest projects. And among these I would tuck in the pleasure and pain of shopping, the pleasure and pain of housekeeping, and the complete pleasure of aimless, frivolous loafing" (*The Arts of Living*, Conde Nast Publications, 1950).

We don't have six lives, though, so we look for balance in the one we have!

And roles are not all we balance. We also balance attitudes and concepts. We balance being cocky and being uncertain, being bored and being busy. We balance our plans for the future and our enjoyment of the moment. We balance making life happen and letting life happen. We balance broad knowledge and specialization. We balance our understanding of God's providence and of our responsibility.

Sometimes, like C. T. Studd, we can have tunnel vision.

We treat life like a subway ride. Sometimes we're so over-whelmed by everything that needs packing, we cancel the trip. How do we deal with the problem of overchoice? The insur-mountable opportunity?

We can set priorities. We can say, "My family comes first—before my church, job, or community." Or we can say that list in a different order.

What do we mean when we say something gets priority? Does it mean simply that it's more important? One friend of mine says in frustration, "My kids are more important than my windows. And if I live by that, I simply never wash win-dows."

Do we mean that a priority item gets 100% of our time? Do we mean the majority—say 51%? Or do we mean it gets more than any other responsibility—say 20%—and all of our other responsibilities get less than 20%?

Do we mean we always put it first in our scheduling? That we take care of it earlier in the day, week, or month—and then move to other items on our responsibility list?

Priority is a good umbrella to aid our balance as we walk life's tightrope, but we need to open that umbrella to make it useful. What do we mean by priorities?

Do-it-first priorities

I set one kind of priorities when I do my dishes. I set do-it-first priorities. First I clear the entire table, then I wash, dry, and put away. Clearing the table is a do-it-first priority. It comes first in the sequence. That's pretty obvious, because the sequence is the most efficient. Imagine first clearing, wash-ing, drying, and putting away the knives, then the forks, then the plates, . . . I'd have lots of wasted motion and use more time. So I opt for the most efficient order.

But do-it-first priorities can also rule by how crucial they are before a deadline. If your family is to fly to a relative's wedding, you have a deadline and a number of tasks to com-plete. They may include: buy tickets, ready clothing, pack, arrange for pet care, stop mail, clean the house, get a tan, and buy new lingerie. If time is limited, you can make choices by how crucial the tasks are. Purchasing tickets is more crucial than purchasing lingerie. Arranging for pet care may be more crucial than cleaning the house. Do-it-first priorities are most useful as they relate to a single goal and deadline: completing the dishes, preparing for a trip. They don't help in deciding how much time you will spend doing dishes and how much time taking trips.

Cut-the-pie priorities

For our varied roles in life we use a different method of setting priorities. We divide the pie of our time into pieces of priorities. Our time is allotted to different roles and tasks. Some of those are biological requirements. We need to spend a certain amount of time eating and sleeping each day. But with other roles, with what's left of the pie, we make choices. We cut different sized pieces for those different roles.

When we think of our time as a pie with some pieces already precommitted, we begin to see the need for choices. It may be useful to draw a pie and draw pieces for how your time is divided. It's not simple, because one task may fulfill two functions. Biking with your children meets your personal need for exercise and is also time spent committed to family. But some general sense of what you feel is an appropriate division might be helpful.

Now look at your pie. Does it conform to what you actually do? You may find it useful to log your time for a couple of weeks to see if your actual pie matches the one you think is appropriate for your calling.

As you look at your pie, ask yourself what in your life you value most. Do your top values get bigger pie pieces? Perhaps the lack of correspondence between your pie and your values will surprise you.

In-case-of-fire priorities

Before you berate yourself for how you divide your time, stop! Your pie might be adequate, because values are a third kind of priority: in-case-of-fire priority. I spend more time on my dishes than on my photo album, but in case of fire I'd save my photographs first. The items on which we spend most time may not necessarily be those we value most. But when a conflict occurs, our in-case-of-fire priorities help us make decisions.

When there is a conflict, the in-case-of-fire priorities win. When you have a sick child and a job to go to, you may need to make an in-case-of-fire priority choice. When your friend needs to talk and you were planning to get groceries, in-case-of-fire priorities may take over.

I have spent more time typing this week than talking one-to-one with my son, even though I value him more. And that's OK. But when he came into my office needing to talk—and I could see it was important to him—the words quit flowing from my fingers and I listened to his. My value priorities took over.

Mary, the mother of three who returned to school, made a set of in-case-of-fire priorities. Her friends and family were higher on the list. So when her father was ill and when a divorced friend needed help packing for a move to a new community, she closed her books. She could make those choices and momentarily let her grades slide because she understood her in-case-of-fire priorities.

Although your in-case-of-fire priorities may not correspond perfectly to your cut-the-pie priorities, you may want to list your values in descending order and check if that makes you want to shift the size of your wedges a little. Knowing your values, your in-case-of-fire priorities, may sometimes be useful in determining what you do first and how you divide your time. But your top in-case-of-fire priority need not always come first or fill the whole pie.

In-case-of-fire priorities do, however, get the time they deserve. I don't spend a high percentage of my time on my photo albums, but I go give them the required time. I keep film in my camera for snapshots. I get it from the closet for capturing precious moments. And once a year I organize my photos into albums for a visual record of that year. I give the job the required time because it is important to me.

If we try to do our best and do it all, we sometimes let sequence priorities preempt value priorities. Some people call this the tyranny of the urgent. Deadlines overrule values. "Sorry, son, I can't listen. I have a deadline to meet." Constant urgency can crowd out the important: "I'm too tired to make love tonight, dear. It's been such a hectic day."

A lawyer who was a time-management buff and carefully scheduled his time to meet career goals was asked where his family fit in his agenda. "Oh, I don't schedule that," he said. "I work that in when I can." What happens in a case like that? Family time vanishes into the mythical future. If we have certain high in-case-of-fire priorities, they need to be part of our sequencing priorities over a span of time. Our in-case-of-fire priorities might not be first in our daily routine, but they need the time they deserve somewhere in our sequence.

When we find that we are not meeting our value priorities because of the tyranny of the urgent, we may need to learn the power and necessity of one two-letter word: no.

When considering a new responsibility, it may be useful to remember that each yes contains a hidden no. If you say yes to a new responsibility, you will be saying no to something currently in your life. Yes may be the right answer. But if you say it, be sure you have an idea of what is falling out the other end of the time-tube into which you are inserting a new role. If may be leisure, it may be sleep, it may be family time, it may be personal time. But you will carve it out of something in your current life.

Dwight Carlson in *Run and Not Be Weary* suggests using tests like these before saying yes:

1) It must be worthy of my time on its own merits.

2) It must be more valuable than any other activity to which I would subsequently have to say no.

3) It must be God's will for me. (How can we know God's will? Living close to him through prayer and Bible reading helps. A sense of our gifts, calling, and goals helps, too.)

Saying no can be surprisingly easy.

An organization to which I belong recently assigned me to a committee without my consent. I was already giving as much time to that organization as I considered appropriate. I stewed and fumed and debated for two days, and finally called the president—nervous and tense. "I'm not sure how I was assigned to chair that committee," I said, "but I am not able to fill that role. I'd really appreciate it if you would find someone else for that position."

Then I waited fearfully for the sky to fall. It didn't. "Oh, yes," she said, "you're writing a slide show for us, aren't you? That takes a lot of time. I'll find someone else for the committee."

I hung up the telephone with relief, and my only regret was that I had agonized for a whole day before daring to dial.

We don't refuse all requests and appointments, but our answer should be in keeping with our calling, our goals, and our priorities. Then we keep a balance.

That balance is maintained, not arrived at. Balance realizes the ephemeral nature of endings. The sands of time keep pouring through our fingers without stopping. Life goes on.

Just as when we walk our point of balance constantly shifts depending on our body position—so with our lives. That balance shifts as we move through different life positions. And it varies for people with different callings and roles.

Mary finds balance by reserving weekends for family. She limits her classwork to weekdays, even if assignments are due Monday mornings. Marilyn has made morning breakfast hour family time because her husband's job requires supper-hour and evening work. For Beth, value priorities meant leaving a social work job she enjoyed when her baby was born. "I found

I just couldn't leave my work at the office, even when I was home evenings," she said. "I wanted more than that for Christy in her early years."

Different people make differing choices to maintain a balance.

But no matter what umbrella we use and how well we open it, there will always be times when we lose our balance and tumble—tumble to the safety net below. We fall sprawling and spinning to the safety net of grace spread by God.

You may have noticed God was conspicuously absent from the list of persons and roles among whom we divide our time. His absence if not my oversight. God doesn't belong anywhere on a priority list—not even at the top. Our responsibility to God goes beyond priorities. He is not one item on the list, but he holds the whole list. Our love, work, and play, our personal lives, relationships, and obligations to institutions, are all part of our relationship to him. In keeping a balance we ask whether our choices are in keeping with his calling for us.

Our obligation to him isn't a segment of our life. It is our whole life. Why do we care for our families? Because there's God. Why do we pursue a career? Because there's God. Why do we work for our church? Because there's God.

To enter God onto our priority list is to make him part of our world, and he is totally other. It is to limit him to one segment of life when he permeates it all.

What does fit on the list, though, is the space we make for our devotional life, our faith life. Where faith life fits is part of our priorities, but not the sum total of our living before God's face. All is lived before his face and out of our relationship to him.

What about our devotional life? We need balance there, too. Our whole pie isn't given to prayer and Bible reading and worship services. We balance work and worship, too. That balance, too, is different for each of us.

But if you find your life running dry, your awareness of God's presence in this world fading, and your desire to serve him shrinking or nonexistent, you may want to go back and look at your in-case-of-fire priorities. Where does your devotional life come in your value priorities? Are your what-comes-first priorities taking over? Do you need to adjust your pie pieces to allow you to open your window to God—to let him in and to guide your other choices?

In the end, no formula will provide balance. In the end, we have a mystical need for his hand to hold ours as we walk the tightrope. In the light of our calling we set our goals, and we walk the tightrope with an open umbrella of priorities, but he is the provider of the rope and the umbrella. He takes us by the hand and leads us. He helps us realize balance instead of obsession with the best.

17

Responding to the Clamor

Tom Peters, coauthor of best-sellers *In Search of Excellence* and *A Passion for Excellence,* has shifted themes and entitled his third book *Thriving on Chaos.* After two books on excellence in business, he begins his third with the startling statement, "There are no excellent companies."

Those of us who haven't written two books on the subject may have a hard time giving up our search and passion for excellence. We may still hear the voices clamoring for it. We may hear them calling for us to do it all. We may hear them asking "yes, but" questions.

"Yes, but doesn't God expect excellence from you? Yes, but you really should do your best for him, shouldn't you? Yes, but won't the gift of good enough make you lazy? Yes, but the world needs excellent Christian politicians, writers, musicians. Yes, but—"

Listen! Newbery Award winning writer Katherine Paterson has on her office wall the motto: "Before the gates of excellence the high gods have placed sweat." But she writes with her back toward that motto. With her back toward it!

Like Katherine Paterson, we can do our work with our backs toward excellence. With Mother Teresa, we can say, "God does not call upon me to be successful, he calls upon me to be faithful."

"Yes, but—"

Listen! At penny carnivals sometimes children are asked to walk 10 feet along a four-inch wide plank, and they easily walk the distance. Then they are given a pair of binoculars, told to look through them backwards, and walk the same board. They lose their balance after the first step or two and step off the plank to regain it. With the binoculars they no longer see the ground accurately and lose their balance. To strive for excellence in everything is to look backward through binoculars.

"Yes, but—"

Listen! In your car is a battery with the power to start it. But if you place a metal bar across the two poles of your battery, you short-circuit it and lose the power to start your car. To achieve respect and worth through excellence is to short-circuit the power of grace.

"Yes, but—"

Listen! Remember Peter? He walked on water! Jesus gave him the power to walk on water! But when Peter took his eyes off Jesus, when he looked at the rolling waves, he started to sink. To be distracted by the clamor for excellence is to take your eyes from Jesus—and start to sink.

"Yes, but—"

Listen! I'd like to ask a few questions of my own. I have three questions for you that precede your yes-but excellence question. Let me ask mine.

Am I a child of God, redeemed through Christ's death and resurrection?

"Yes, but—"

Am I, through Christ, good enough for God's purposes in my life?

"Yes, but—"

Am I cooperating with him in fulfilling those purposes?
"Yes, but—"

I'm sorry, we've just run out of time. Those three questions are enough to fill a lifetime. I've no time left for the excellence question.

"Yes, but—"

I'm sorry. I have no time left to talk. I have work and worship on my agenda.

The voices cease.

In the end, I do not answer the voices, they simply stop talking. I have learned what to do when I can't do it all.

What do I do . . .

When I plan to run
and can only crawl,
When instead of succeeding
I find I fall,
When my rate of growth
is at a stall,
And in perfection's path
I find a wall?

What do I do . . .

When I can't do it all?
I listen in silence
for my Father's call.
I try what he asks
whether large or small.
Then I turn my face
to his risen Son,
And I hear him whisper,
"It's all been done."